Change Your Perspective, Change Your Life

Gradient Publication

Published by Gradient Publication, 2023.

CHANGE YOUR PERSPECTIVE, CHANGE YOUR LIFE

First edition. September 20, 2023.

Copyright © 2023 Gradient Publication.

Written by Gradient Publication.

Table of Contents

Change Your Perspective, Change Your Life

Empowering Yourself Through Change

What You'll Learn

1. Learn how to use the change acceleration process as a model for change leadership
2. Transition an entire organisation from a current state to a future state to sustain effective change
3. Utilise employee engagement to combat resistance to change
4. Understand the difference between a change process and a transition process
5. Create an action plan to manage the transition
6. Understand and eliminate your resistances to change
7. Understand the emotions that may be getting in your way

About

Even though change is a constant in life, humans frequently fight or dread it. Although change is necessary for our development and growth, we frequently struggle during the many stages of a shift.

Participants will be prompted to reflect on their own habits, resistances, and emotions as they progress through the transformation process through slides and reflection exercises. We will be better able to survive any change if we have a deeper understanding of our own emotions and hurdles during the process.

This Book will provide you some basic yet useful techniques and principles to effectively flourish during a transition, whether you need to manage change on a personal level or assist a team member, family member, friend, etc.

Who Should Take This Course

1. Anyone who wishes to cope with change more effectively.
2. Managers and group leaders
3. Parents who desire to support the development of their children via change
4. Those who want to learn how to lead individuals, teams and organisations through long lasting, organisational change.

Introduction

It can be exceedingly challenging to bring about change in our life, even positive change: breaking habits becomes harder as we age; doing something repeatedly becomes tougher; and changing perspectives becomes harder the longer we have a perspective. This qualifies as a human quality. However, we also have an inclination to think that changing will be simple and possible in a short amount of time.

Due to our desire for rapid gratification, many of us give up on or abandon initiatives when they take too long. Unfortunately, our drive for immediate gratification is precisely what prevents us from being successful in our attempts to bring about change. Understanding that change takes time and necessitates patience throughout the process is the key to creating change that endures.

When Will Change Occur?

You may have heard that it takes 18 days to break a habit. You may also be familiar with the terms 21 and 28 days. The truth is that the length of time needed to effect lasting change varies greatly depending on the person, the change, and the situation.

This subject was especially covered in a study1 by University College London psychologist Phillippa Lally. She discovered that it often took 66 days for people who were trying to create new behaviours for them to become automatic. In other words, it usually took 912 weeks for people to experience a significant improvement in their life. However, the range covered anything from an expedited 18-day turnaround to a demanding 245-day period. Even though it may sound depressing, change takes time. I bring this up to emphasise my point.

Keep the following in mind as you start your journey toward a better, healthier way of life:

One large change requires many small ones first: Every large change always requires a lot of lesser adjustments. Consider this: if changing to a healthy diet is your only change, you probably need to make a lot of other changes as well. It might be necessary for you to consume fewer fried foods, smaller portions, more veggies, etc.

Extremes Never Work. It is common for us to want to go from everything to nothing when we want to make significant changes in our lives, or the opposite. Consider Bob as an example. Bob wanted to become in shape but has never worked out. He made the decision to work out for an hour each day of the week to achieve this.

Within a few weeks, Bob lost interest in exercising, began to feel exhausted, and gave up. He overexerted himself too soon. On the other hand, Bob would have had a better chance of sticking with the plan and of the change lasting if he had eased into a fitness program by beginning with two half-hour workouts per week and then gradually adding workout days and time over a few months.

Gradually implementing change makes it seem more achievable and less daunting.

Our Success Is Fueled by Small Changes Requirement: We will never feel satisfied if we set out to achieve a big change but overlook every little step we take along the road. We can, however, feel as though we are progressing if we make modest improvements and acknowledge our accomplishments in mastering each one. This then spurs us on to continue making small adjustments, which ultimately aids in completing the larger alteration.

Keep these tips in mind for the next 25 weeks to help you stay grounded in reality and achieve your objectives for a happy, healthy life.

The 25 Small Changes Program's

The 25 Tiny Changes Program aims to promote small but significant lifestyle adjustments that, over time, will result in a dramatic shift toward a happier, healthier way of life. Simple as it seems, the concept is that by making one tiny change every week for 25 weeks, you'll be happier and healthier at the end of the year. Two goals guided the creation of this book:

1) Although you can make numerous adjustments, the 25 suggestions in this book will have the biggest influence on your capacity to lead a happier, healthier life.

2) You have the option to gradually incorporate significant changes over time by giving yourself a year to construct this lifestyle, which increases the likelihood that they will endure in the long run.

Each of the 25 weekly modifications is explained along with a "Roadmap for Success" that offers advice and suggestions to assist you in putting it into practice. The little adjustment will have been worked on by the end of each week, or at the very least, you will be adept enough to incorporate it into your normal practice.

You will continue to put the adjustments from the prior weeks into practice as you move on to a new change each following week. You'll have mastered 25 adjustments by the end of the year, which will ultimately result in your pleasure and well-being. Even though making one of these tiny changes per week will make them easier to maintain and, most importantly, more durable, small changes still demand some effort.

Additionally, I've included an Extra Credit section for some of the modifications. You can strengthen whatever lifestyle adjustments you may already be making by putting the advice and suggestions under Extra Credit to use. Pay special attention to the advice given under Roadmap for Success if you are unfamiliar with the modification. If you eventually master the change to a high level, go back and try the Extra Credit.

I gave you Tools and Resources in Part III to use throughout the next 25 weeks. You can find tools to help you here, such as trackers and templates. I strongly advise using these to help you stay inspired and concentrated while working out.

A Wide-Reaching Approach

It takes more than healthy food and exercise to lead a happy, healthy life. You have a lot of obstacles in life to get beyond. Diane will be used as an example. A few years ago, Diane used to routinely go to her bedroom to find relief from her tension headaches and migraines.

She had a weak immune system and frequently contracted colds and sinus infections. She also didn't feel energetic or tired enough to do anything. She needed a solution more than anyone else. Diane appeared to put her health first on the surface.

She was the go-to person for friends and family when it came to making good decisions since she ate sensibly, kept a balanced diet, and was passionate about excellent nutrition. Diane had a hard time understanding why she was feeling so awful. I learned that Diane had a young child, a hard career, and little free time as I dug more into her life. Diane had improved in one aspect of healthy living—her diet—but she had neglected others, such as stress reduction, preventing disease, and exercise.

As a result, Diane's life lost its equilibrium, which ultimately made her health problems worse.

Diane's health problems may, fortunately, be curable. Her health significantly improved when we showed her how to control her stress, set aside some alone time, and exercise. This demonstrates that maintaining a healthy lifestyle requires more than just following a balanced diet and engaging in regular exercise.

Health and happiness benefits of a lifestyle

Changing to a happier, healthier lifestyle has many benefits. The following are some of the primary advantages you could anticipate:

A More Satisfying and Rewarding Life. If you have greater energy, physical stamina, and mental stability, you will be able to live life to the fullest, give your best effort at work, and feel amazing in every way.

Improved Prognosis. Your outlook will be brighter and more upbeat, and this will come through in your interpersonal interactions, career, and other facets of your life.

Making informed decisions, staying active, and feeling energised at any age are all aspects of a healthy lifestyle. You'll feel and appear younger as a result.

Self-esteem. Taking care of oneself not only improves your physical health, but also your emotional health. Your sense of self-worth and confidence will consequently rise.

Natural Safety Net. Living a healthy lifestyle today will eliminate the need for punitive acts in the future. Making your health a priority helps keep your mind sharp and prevent diseases like diabetes, cancer, and heart disease. As a result, you will age more gradually.

Gaining More Control Over Your Life. You'll be more equipped, both physically and psychologically, to make lemonade when life offers you lemons. Life's unforeseen obstacles won't overwhelm you as much, and you'll be better equipped to handle them.

Sensitivity has increased. This tactic will aid in the development of a clear understanding of your options. You'll be able to tune into your body and mind with this increased awareness and discover what they require to perform at their best.

The 25 Small Changes Program approaches health and happiness from a whole-person perspective. You will research topics including diet and nutrition, exercise and prevention, mental health, and green living throughout the course of the next 25 weeks. To have a healthy lifestyle, they are all essential.

A marker designating the area of change being addressed will be noticeable at the start of each week. You won't ever discuss the same topic twice in a row thanks to the improvements that were necessary. This will keep you motivated and interested, get you closer to a holistically happier, healthier way of living, provide you more time for areas that are difficult, and help you achieve your goals. The following icons can be seen:

The Weekly Changes Checklist, which summarises all the changes from the previous week so you can be sure to keep adopting them into your way of life, can be found at the end of each week.

The 25 Week Span That Follows

You'll feel happier and healthier than you do now when the 52-week program is over. You'll have more energy, learn more about what it takes to be healthy, and, most importantly, learn how to live a healthy lifestyle.

The 25 modifications might not always be quick and simple to sustain. There will be times when it will be difficult because of your schedule or your obligations in life, but this is just a fact of life. Don't let mistakes make you feel insufficient. Sometimes in life, we must make sacrifices. When those less healthy moments arise, keep in mind that tomorrow is a new day and that those unwholesome feelings are only momentary. Try to keep them brief, and start each day with fresh inspiration and fresh eyes.

Since 25 Small Changes will always give you the building blocks for a better and healthier life, you should frequently visit it. And think about making 25 Small Changes an annual endeavour. There are no secrets involved; this is a simple method that will make you forever happy and healthy.

Choose Your Own Path

This journey is entirely yours, even though I've planned 25 Small Changes to last a year and have a predetermined course. You should modify how you utilise this book to suit your needs. If one is exceptionally simple or has already become a part of your life, feel free to do it right now. However, I strongly advise waiting a week before making any additional adjustments.

If you choose, you may read this book in a different order than chronologically. However, there are two things I want to highlight: Give your changes time to stick, and no matter the time range you select, make sure you execute all 25 modifications because they are designed to complement one another.

Baseline for Success

I want you to take some time to consider where you are right now before you start the 25 Small Changes. If you succeed in doing this, you will have a starting point for the following 25 weeks. By completing a SheerBalance online assessment, you may determine your baseline. Similar to the 25 Small Changes Program, the examination examines every aspect of your health, including diet and nutrition, exercise and prevention, mental health, and green living. You'll receive a brief overview of your performance in each of these areas at the conclusion of the exam so you can get started with the program.

It's critical to realise that the evaluation is based more on factors in your control than those outside of your control. Your lifestyle decisions are more important to the inquiries than your medical history or genetic make-up.

Guarantee Your Success

Your ability to control your expectations will be put to the test during the following 25 weeks, and it will be crucial to your success. You'll be more motivated and able to embrace the upcoming 25 weeks of transformation if you maintain a positive mindset and set reasonable goals for the procedure and yourself.

1) Accept the fact that this will be how you live. The 25 Small Changes Program is not a weight-loss plan, exercise regimen, or health panacea. It is essentially a new way of living or a lifestyle. Your success depends on your ability to recognize that maintaining a healthy lifestyle requires a holistic approach—one you fully embrace and one you respect, nurture, and promote.

2. Recognize the continual nature of the process. This program, which will span 25 weeks, is designed to assist you in making significant changes that will last. Consider this a process or, even better, a journey as a result. You can enjoy the process better if you are aware that your path will require some time and patience.

What This Book Is Missing

Over the next 25 weeks, you'll acquire some incredibly useful advice and put it into practice, but there are some subjects we won't be covering.

Alcohol: While moderate alcohol usage may improve your health, reducing your risk of heart disease, excessive alcohol use can be detrimental to your well-being. Drinking too much has been related to a number of health problems, including liver illness, memory loss, learning difficulties, vitamin and mineral deficiencies, osteoporosis, pancreatic problems, and irregular sleep patterns. Women should not consume more than one drink each day, while males should not consume more than two.

Smoking: Smoking is really unhealthy for you. Lung cancer, heart disease, and emphysema have all been linked to smoking. Additionally, it can seriously harm your skin and speed up ageing. It is advised that you begin a smoking cessation program as soon as possible if you are a smoker.

Drugs: It is typically advised to reduce your dependence on drugs and avoid using them recreationally. All drugs, including illicit narcotics, medicines prescribed for medical purposes, and opioids, have the power to alter how our bodies function. If your body doesn't require these drugs, they could harm your heart, brain, and other vital organs.

I advise you to stop engaging in any harmful habits you may have, such as excessive drinking, smoking, or drug use. You should get help right away if you think you could have an alcohol or drug addiction issue.

3. Be practical. Set realistic goals for both the program and for yourself. Do not overburden oneself with obligations. Everybody is different, so you might find that some adjustments are easier for you to implement than others, just as some changes will be more enjoyable for you than others. Don't let this bring you down. Instead, give yourself time to adjust to each change, and let the accomplishment of each week motivate you to the next.

4) Keep undesirables outdoors. Avoid thinking or speaking negatively. Think positively and consider all the wonderful outcomes of this course. Think about the advantages rather than the drawbacks, such as "I'll feel great," "I'll prevent the onset of disease," "I'll feel more connected to my family and friends," and "I'll feel less stressed."

5. Make a decision. You can choose to look for health and happiness. You wanted it for some reason deep down. Keep your attention on the word "I want to" and disregard the words "I have to," "I should," and "I'm supposed to."

(6). Be Faithful and Forgiving: You won't become healthy just by reading 25 Small Changes. But moving forward will. Be devoted and aware that your actions, successes, and health are ultimately in your power. But in the meantime, be kind to yourself if you mess up or go backward. Be aware that life will periodically make it tough for you to keep to your goals, and that you will experience both good and bad days. As you go through this process, be kind to yourself.

7) Understand that this isn't rigorous science. Maintaining a healthy lifestyle is not difficult or complicated, despite appearances to the contrary. Once you know how to do it, leading a healthy lifestyle may be easy to undertake and is really simply a matter of common sense. Even if it might not feel that way right now, The 25 Small Changes will show you how to enjoy life to the fullest while improving your health and happiness.

Now that you are fully aware of your condition and what it will take for your 52-week journey to be successful, let's get going.

Consume During The First Week!

"Water is the life force that sustains and powers all of nature." Despite the fact that water is not a significant source of vitamins or minerals, it is nevertheless vital to your nutrition and general health. Your body is 60 to 70 percent water, so it is essential for regular physiological function that you replenish it every day.

Water aids in nutrient delivery to your cells and aids in digestion. It maintains a moist environment for the ear, nose, and throat tissues and lubricates joints, cushions essential organs and tissues, and cushions vital organs and tissues. Your blood is kept healthy, your skin remains supple and stretchable, and you have the ability to cool off when you become overheated (particularly when working out). Maintaining proper hydration is the key to receiving all of these advantages. It also helps the body's cleansing process.

An Approach To Success

Any liquid, including milk, juice, and sports drinks, can generally be thought of as a kind of hydration. Contrarily, water is by far the greatest option because it has no calories, is easily absorbed, and is linked to several health benefits. It is advised that you concentrate on increasing the amount of water you consume each day as a result.

Decide What You Need Everyone differs in what they require from water. Your specific needs will be determined by a number of variables, such as the local temperature and humidity, the amount of daily exercise and activity, your general health, and, for women, whether or not you are pregnant or nursing. Although there are a few popular ways to determine how much water you should consume each day, I prefer to use your weight as a guide.

Water consumption should equal your weight in pounds divided by two. For instance, you should try to drink 75 ounces of water per day if you weigh 150 pounds. Make use of this strategy as a base. Afterward, increase your daily water intake if any of the following apply:

Exercise: For every 20 minutes of exercise, consume an additional eight ounces of water.

Alcohol: Substitute an equal amount of water for each alcoholic beverage.

Travel: Increase your water consumption by eight ounces for every hour of flight time.

region: Drink an additional sixteen ounces of water if you live in a dry area.

Eight more ounces of water should be consumed before each feeding if you are breastfeeding.

Increase your water intake when expecting by eight ounces. Drinking enough water to avoid dehydration and make sure your pee isn't too coloured or perfumed is a good general rule of thumb.

2. Spread It Out: Distributing your daily water consumption is the best course of action. When you first get up, drink an eight-ounce glass of water every hour.

3. Before Meals and Snacks: Before each meal and snack, sip a glass of water. By filling you full before meals and ensuring that you obtain the recommended quantity of water throughout the day, this can help you prevent overeating.

Flavor-Infused Water And Flavoured Beverages

Preservatives, artificial additives, sugar, and extra calories that you don't need are regularly found in goods like Vitamin Water, Life Water, Gatorade, and other flavoured waters. Additionally, artificial sweetener-containing beverages often contain substances that are, at best, dubious. 100% juice offers vitamins and minerals as well as other nutrients, although it is often heavy in sugar and calories. So it is preferable to hydrate with water, club soda, or sodium-free seltzer.

Constantly have a BPA-free water bottle with you. Invest in a BPA-free or stainless steel water bottle rather than drinking from a glass. Carry it with you all day long and fill it as necessary. By doing this instead of buying water in bottles, you will be encouraged to drink water frequently, have access to water throughout the day, and save money.

Make a reminder: Make a reminder system while you are just getting started. Set up an hourly reminder to drink water if you heavily rely on technology, such as a smartphone, iPhone, or Outlook calendar. You won't likely need the reminder once drinking enough water each day becomes a habit. But initially, it ought to aid with memory retention and keep you on track.

Be Sincere: The value of water has already been mentioned. However, if drinking regular water makes you sick, consider one of these alternatives: Consume natural, unsweetened, decaffeinated beverages like herbal tea or club soda without salt.

To your water or club soda, add a squeeze of lime or some lemon juice. Give your water a fruit or veggie infusion. Raspberries, oranges, melon, lemons, and limes are some of the greatest fruits to choose from, while cucumbers make a delicious vegetable infusion. The fruit or vegetable is cut into pieces and placed in a pitcher of water. For the fruit or vegetable to properly infuse the water, leave the pitcher out for a few hours.

Have you heard of it?

Water is more vital to our bodies than food. A person may go four to six weeks without eating but only three to five days without water, depending on the situation, the temperature, and the level of physical activity.

Extra Credit Are you now well hydrated? Your water will be improved by adding a filter. Use a water filtration system to purify the tap water in your home. This will assist in removing any contaminants that may be present in your water supply, such as heavy metals, sediments, agricultural pollutants, industrial and commercial pollutants, and even pharmaceutical residues. Carry a water bottle with a filter with you when you're on the run. On the market, there are a few reliable names like Clear2Go, Water Bobble, Canteen, or Watergeeks.

Get Good Sleep!

The importance of obtaining adequate sleep for your health should go without saying. When we get enough sleep, which also supports and strengthens the immune system, improves memory retention and cognitive ability, and balances hormones, we feel and look our best.

We may experience issues with our mental and emotional health when we don't receive enough. We may feel headaches, exhaustion, irritation, and a short attention span in the short term. The long-term repercussions of inadequate sleep, however, include memory loss, sadness, high blood pressure and irregular heartbeats, slowed metabolism, which can result in weight gain or diabetes, and greater susceptibility to health issues.

Have you heard of it?

All three tragedies—the 1986 Chernobyl nuclear accident, the 1989 Exxon Valdez oil leak off the coast of Alaska, and the Challenger space shuttle disaster—were deemed to be the result of human error, with sleep deprivation playing a part in each of them.

An Approach To Success

Studies show that we need seven to eight hours of sleep each night for our health and wellbeing. Give yourself the gift of sleep every night; it will benefit you greatly. Here are some suggestions to help you get the recommended amount of zzz's:

Make your bedroom the best setting for rest: If your surroundings don't support sleep, you might find it easier to wake up frequently throughout the night, which would disturb your sleep cycle and the crucial REM state. Think about the following to create the ideal sleeping environment:

Lighting: Loud lights from outside or inside your bedroom may awaken you. For better sleep, keep your bedroom dark. Dim the clock lights and use nightlights in the toilets and hallways. For protection from intrusive outdoor light, use drapes or shades.

Loud noises should not be allowed in your bedroom. Invest in a white noise machine to assist hide the worst of the noise if your room's location makes it difficult to escape it.

Use opulent bedding and wear soft, non-restrictive sleepwear to encourage a peaceful night's sleep. Temperature: Extreme heat or cold when sleeping may have an impact on REM sleep patterns. Additionally, when we are sleeping or in REM, we lose some of our ability to manage how warm we are. It is crucial to maintain a temperature in your bedroom set that is neither too hot nor too cold.

Humidity: Much like extreme heat or cold, extreme dryness or humidity may make it difficult for us to sleep. To provide moisture to the dry air in your environment, use a humidifier. Use a dehumidifier to reduce some of the extreme moisture in your environment if it is, however, extremely humid.

Make a sleep routine since regular, consistent sleep schedules are essential for healthy sleep patterns. To manage your biological clock and circadian rhythms (rhythms natural to human eating and sleeping patterns), go to bed and wake up at the same time each day. Determine how much earlier you need to go to bed in order to make up the time if you are currently sleeping less than the required seven hours. You can gradually alter your habit by putting yourself to bed fifteen minutes earlier each night until you've gotten the seven to eight hours you need.

Workouts to improve time management If you exercise too much soon before bed, it could be difficult to fall asleep. The best times to work out are in the morning or late at night. If you work out after work, try to finish by early evening to give your body enough time to unwind and get ready for bed.

Create a bedtime schedule: Create a relaxing bedtime routine to help your body and mind get ready for sleep. Here are some suggestions: Sip some herbal tea without caffeine. The Yogi Tea "Bedtime Tea" is pretty good. Take a bath with lavender oil to relax and cleanse your mind. Listen to music that is calming and serene.

Before going to bed, turn the lights down. This aids in alerting the brain that bedtime is approaching. Keep a journal where you can jot down your thoughts and upcoming assignments. Make a list of everything you want to accomplish so you can put it aside and unwind.

Avoid using sleep inhibitors: Avoid using caffeine and other brain stimulants in the late afternoon. These might make it difficult for you to get asleep or stay asleep all night. Although each person is different, it's a good general rule to avoid stimulants after 2:30 pm. The best way to determine how stimulants affect you and your sleep patterns is to pay attention to how you personally react to them. Remember that chocolate and sweets both include sugar and caffeine.

Limit alcohol consumption: While alcohol can help you unwind and fall asleep, it can also interfere with your sleep cycle and prevent you from getting a good night's rest. After consuming alcohol, your sleep cycles tend to be shorter, which makes it easier for you to wake up in the middle of the night. As a result, you miss out on both necessary REM sleep and deeper, more restorative sleep.

Smoking: Smoking is bad for your overall health as well as your sleep patterns. Smokers often have mild sleep cycles, which cuts down on the amount of time spent in REM sleep. Smokers frequently wake up because three to four hours after going to bed, the body experiences nicotine withdrawal.

Eating: It's ideal to finish your meal no later than nine hours before you want to go to bed. If not, it's possible that having a functional digestive system will keep you awake. Make sure your meal has a healthy balance of lean protein and complex carbohydrates. Avoid consuming too much fat or simple carbohydrates (such as sugar and foods prepared with refined wheat). If you eat things that make you uncomfortable, cause acid reflux, or give you a lot of gas, you won't be able to sleep at night.

Fluids: It's advisable to avoid consuming a lot of liquids, especially water, two to three hours before going to bed unless you want to have to get up numerous times during the night to use the bathroom. Ensure that you consume the majority of your liquids in the morning.

Have you heard of it?

In terms of the amount of time without sleep, the record is 18 days, 21 hours, and 40 minutes. This record was established after a lengthy rocking chair session. Hallucinations, paranoia, blurry vision, slurred speech, and problems with memory and focus were all noted by the record holder.

Avoid The Sofa

There was once a species called "humans." They hunted and foraged in addition to walking and running. They were engaged in their usual activities. But as technology developed, the demand for this level of effort decreased, and people turned into a more sedentary species.

Dan Buettner outlines how those who live the longest do so in circumstances that require them to move continuously and without pausing in his book The Blue Zones. By walking to the store, gardening, using the stairs, and other activities, these people stay active all day long.

Staying active has several advantages beyond only prolonging your life; it also significantly improves your quality of life. Regular exercise lowers the risk of metabolic syndrome and type 2 diabetes, both of which are risk factors for heart disease. It can also improve your general well-being, strengthen your bones and muscles, and lower your risk of developing certain malignancies. Finally, protecting yourself as you age is helpful.

Simply said, exercising regularly can prolong your youth and improve your general health.

An Approach To Success

It will be simpler to keep an active body, which is how it was meant to be utilised, the more active you are. This transformation does not entail going to the gym for an hour each day or walking three miles. It entails deciding to move as opposed to remaining still.

You must discover where the prospects for activity are located in order to complete this adjustment properly. Even simple decisions can have a significant impact over time.

Take This Highway: One of the simplest and most effective ways to add activity to your day is to go for a walk. Simply by taking a few additional steps here and there, you can add a mile or more. Pick one of the following times to go for a walk:

Consider walking to work if you live in a city rather than taking public transportation. Get off the train or bus a few stops early so you can walk the last ten to fifteen minutes of your trip if your distance is too great to finish on foot.

Walking your dog: Dogs need to go on two walks a day, at least. Start walking the dog instead of letting him out as normal. Consider buying a dog if you enjoy animals but don't already have one to encourage you to go outside. Labradors and Border Collies are among the breeds that are more energetic.

Performing Tasks: Instead of driving, ride a bike or go for a stroll to the neighbouring store. While transporting your items and travelling to and from your destination, you will be on the move.

Parking: Try to park further from a building's entrance, even though it would appear more convenient to do so. beginning or finishing the day: Take a stroll before breakfast and/or after dinner, or make multiple trips to and from your automobile each day to cover a significant amount of ground rapidly. It's better than nothing, even if you can only fit in five to ten minutes. Walking after dinner is particularly advantageous since it promotes digestion and reduces satiety before bed.

Play a Lunchtime Game: Make your lunch more active rather than eating at your desk or heading out to a restaurant with pals. Take a walk and talk business with a coworker. execute errands. You might do some shopping.

If you sit at your desk all day at work, get up every hour and stretch. Instead of calling a coworker over the phone to speak with them, go to their office down the hall. Take the stairs to a different floor to obtain a cup of coffee or use the restroom rather than using the facilities on your floor.

Watching TV is one of the least physically active things you may engage in and is also one of the main causes of a sedentary lifestyle. Simply decide to make TV time more active rather than fully giving it up.

Laundry: Switch loads from the washer to the dryer during the commercial breaks of your favourite programs.

Despite the fact that the noise will prevent you from vacuuming while watching TV, now is the ideal time to dust, organise, and clean the living room and other neighbouring areas.

Cardio: If you have the money, invest in some cardio equipment that you can use at home to exercise while binge-watching your favourite programs. Quieter treadmill alternatives include cross trainers, stationary bikes, stairmasters, and elliptical trainers.

Floating exercises You can easily start strength training if you don't want to spend money on expensive cardio equipment. It's easy to perform floor exercises like sit-ups, push-ups, and others while watching television.

Get up straight: For climbs and descents of seven storeys or less, always use the stairs rather than the elevator or escalator, no matter how enticing they may seem. Take the elevator if the height or decrease is greater on the following levels; otherwise, take the stairs.

Utilise Yourself Do your own housework and other activities rather than hiring someone to do them for you. Clean up your home. disinfect it. Create a garden. Create a shed. You'll become more active as you complete more autonomous work.

As soon as you can, get up. This includes when you're on the phone, working on a computer, watching TV, browsing the web, unwinding in a waiting room, or taking the bus.

A good time Enjoying physical activities that don't seem like exercise is one of the simplest ways to stay active. In the winter, skate on the ice in the park. In the summer, wander along the shore. Birds should be avoided in the spring. Take part in one or two enjoyable activities each week to raise your total level of activity. Take their lead when you have the chance to interact with others. Instead of going to a play or movie, go hiking. Wander aimlessly. Instead of lying in the sun, go for a walk on the beach. Start dancing with a friend.

Disconnect because technology is mostly to blame for our sedentary lifestyles. For instance, when changing stations, the remote control has essentially taken the place of our legs. When shovelling snow, the snow blower has taken the place of our arms and legs. Leaf raking is no longer necessary thanks to the leaf blower. Select manual methods whenever possible.

Have You Heard?

The World Health Organization claims that a substantial underlying factor in disease, mortality, and disability is inactivity. The cause of more than two million fatalities per year is physical inactivity.

In other words, practically anything is now possible for us to perform, either actively or passively. When given a choice, pick the first option. It will lift your spirits.

Have You Heard?

Simply spending two minutes each time you go up or down stairs will lower your overall cholesterol and raise your "good" cholesterol. According to studies, those who ascend 55 flights a week have a lesser risk of developing heart issues. Over the course of a year, even just two flights of stairs each day can result in a six-pound weight loss.

Extra Points

Are you now a trustworthy performer? Get a pedometer and take the 10,000-step challenge to go further. Over the past few years, experts have advised walking 10,000 steps each day to make sure you're receiving enough exercise. Keep track of how many steps you take each day to see if they add up.

Keep A Food Journal

There is a tendency for many people to overstate how healthy their diets are. For instance, they might not know what a truly healthy diet entails. Second, it's a natural human propensity to recall healthier decisions like skipping the donut or only eating half of the huge dinner but rapidly forgetting less healthy ones. But keeping track of your food is a great method to avoid these blunders, enabling you to maintain a balanced diet and make healthy decisions.

When you record your daily food intake, you become more accountable for your choices. Simply monitoring your food intake might act as a constant reminder that you are actively choosing to put your health and wellbeing first. By tracking your eating patterns, you can learn how your emotions and feelings affect how you interact with food. You'll discover which foods make you feel a certain way and begin to see trends in the hours of the day you frequently overeat or indulge. Additionally, if you're trying to make healthy dietary changes, keeping a food journal will let you monitor your progress.

You can have a better grasp of the nutritional value of the foods you eat by maintaining a food record. You'll start to understand where your calories come from and what your meals and snacks are made of nutritionally. Knowing this will make modifying your diet as needed easier. By meticulously noting your meals, journaling also lessens the possibility of subjectivity or selective memory. Because even a half of a chocolate chip cookie gets captured, there is no room for fluff-offs. The increased accountability will make you far more likely to reconsider eating unhealthy foods.

Even though some dietary recommendations, like obtaining enough fibre, are applicable to everyone, there are numerous dietary needs that vary from person to person, such as food allergies or intolerances. By keeping a food journal, you can learn more about how your body reacts to various foods and what might make you feel bloated, worn out, or sick to your stomach. Using the information shown here, you can create a more tailored eating plan that is healthier and more in line with your preferences and needs.

A Strategy For Success

Although it may seem challenging at first, keeping a meal journal will become second nature as you get the hang of it:

Writing instructions for eating and drinking. Keep track of everything you eat and drink, including how much of each, from an orange to a cookie to a glass of water. This will help you choose the foods that will best sate your cravings on an emotional as well as physical level. To determine how well-balanced your meals and snacks are, use this as a standard. Include the number of servings and your daily calorie intake. As many people have a propensity to underestimate their portion sizes, you might wish to utilise measuring cups, measuring spoons, or food scales to accurately record your consumption, especially at the beginning. Not least, don't forget to list the days you indulge because knowing this information is just as important as knowing the days you behave well.

Appetite. On a scale of 0 to 5, where 0 represents "extremely hungry" and 5 represents "extremely full," rate your level of hunger. Never allow yourself to experience a hunger or fullness level of 0 or 5. Try to stay between 1 and 4 to maintain your physical, mental, and emotional well-being. It promotes moderation, independence, and acceptance of your decisions by raising your awareness of the how, why, what, and when you consume.

Keep a notebook where you may record how you feel before, during, and after meals and snacks to keep track of your mental and physical health. Before and during meals, be conscious of your physical and emotional state. How did you react when you first felt hungry? Did you have a specific idea in mind? Have you ever felt stressed? Depressed? Happy? Relaxed? Bored? To understand what drives you to eat, make a mental note of your feelings. Are you really hungry? Do you turn to food to fill emptiness in your life? Is it necessary to eat when we celebrate? By noting these sensations, you can distinguish between physical and emotional hunger.

A Manual For Journaling

How you journal will depend on your personal interests. In essence, you want to choose a medium that is easiest for you to work with. You ought to share some of your food journals online, in my opinion. Visit several online resources, such as Fitday and MyFoodDiary. There are many applications available for the iPhone and other devices that you can download to quickly keep track of your daily caloric intake.

The bulk of these systems are quite good at assessing numerical data, like the number of calories you consume and how much of your diet is made up of fat, carbohydrates, and protein. The most practical way to record the more qualitative information, such as feelings and emotions, might be to journal them in a notebook. To make sure you capture all the relevant information, you can organise your notebook using the food journal template from Part III—Tools and Resources.

False Curiosity Instincts

We frequently think we are hungry when we really are not. Dietitian and health specialist Brooke Joanna Benlifer lists the following as the primary causes of people mistaking their hunger for other things:

Lack of a Proper Nutrient Balance: If you eat a large meal that is rich in simple carbohydrates but low in fibre, protein, or healthy fats—all of which help you feel satisfied—your blood sugar may decrease. In this circumstance, eat a balanced, healthy meal, such as a piece of fresh fruit and a cup of unsalted nuts.

Emotional hunger is a classic indicator of boredom, anxiety, tension, and loneliness. Try taking a stroll, talking to a friend, meditating, listening to music, or chewing gum if you notice these triggers. If this condition persists, learn coping mechanisms for the emotions that are causing the fake hunger.

It's probable that your failure to get the recommended seven hours of sleep each night is what's causing your hunger. If so, take a brief 10-minute walk around the block to increase blood flow to your brain and clear your head. A cup of green tea, which is high in antioxidants and contains less caffeine than coffee, is another choice, as is an energising and wholesome snack. Even a few slow, deep breaths can help you feel less worn out.

Hunger as a Result of Thirst: Hunger and thirst are frequently confused. Try drinking a glass or two of water to see if you are truly thirsty or just slightly dehydrated. If you identify with the second group, begin to understand the emotional components of eating and develop the ability to distinguish between real and fake hunger. Create countermeasures for when your personal triggers threaten to overwhelm you by analysing them.

When and How to Journal

You are advised to keep a daily journal. You'll ensure that you remember nothing and are as accurate as you can be by doing this. If you wait until the end of the day or even a few hours after you eat or drink, it is easier to forget the specifics.

The News, You Say?

Researchers found that dieters who kept food diaries six days a week and recorded every meal dropped twice as much weight as those who did so just sometimes or never. The study was published in the American Journal of Preventive Medicine.

Extra Credit

Do you currently have an interest in writing about food? start a fitness journal. Keeping track of your activity can help you see both sides of the equation because the ratio of calories consumed to calories spent is a crucial aspect in weight reduction and weight management. Record the nature, extent, and length of your work. This can also be followed online using some of the resources mentioned before.

Consider the Glass to be Half Full

Positivity can be a wonderful personal trait and a huge help in living an ideal life. A "half-full glass" attitude gives the impression that one is assured, relaxed, and at ease with oneself. They don't let things bother them, thus they almost certainly make good company. But the best thing about a positive outlook is that it's beneficial to your health.

According to numerous studies, those with a happy view on life are more likely to remain healthy and live longer. Having a positive outlook can lower blood pressure, the likelihood of developing hypertension and heart disease, as well as the risk of dying too young.

A Harvard and Boston University study found that people who were pessimistic had a greater than double the risk of developing heart disease than people who were optimistic. Another study found that optimists had a 14% lower risk of dying from any cause and a 9% lower risk of developing heart disease than their pessimistic peers. People with high degrees of "cynical hostility" had a 16% higher chance of passing away compared to all other groups.

Everyone needs optimism to go through therapy or surgery and recover fully, particularly those who have been diagnosed with a chronic illness. An optimistic person was only half as likely as a pessimist to need rehospitalization within six months of surgery, according to a study that examined the relationship between optimism and particular medical conditions.

One's emotional wellbeing is also improved by learning to reframe one's mental processes in a more positive manner. Positive people are better at managing stress and are more inclined to persevere through challenging conditions. According to studies, having an optimistic outlook can lessen the symptoms of depression and suffering.

Typically, optimists have faith in their own abilities and enjoy making predictions that turn out well. Additionally, they are more willing to take chances in order to fill their lives with more rewarding experiences.

Consequently, optimists are more likely to succeed, perform well, and accomplish their goals. Failures are only seen as minor obstacles that may be easily overcome. Pessimists, on the other hand, are more inclined to give up easily, are less likely to persevere through difficult circumstances, and are more likely to achieve poorly.

An Approach To Success

Being upbeat and cheerful doesn't need to be unrealistic or blind to the difficulties of life. Instead, it entails changing your perspective to one that is more useful and positive. Here are a few advices:

Discreet Self-Talk Even while it's typical for us to be harder on ourselves than on others, pessimism is basically based on negative self-talk. Filtering, which is when you emphasise the negative and minimise the positive, personalising, which is when you automatically assign blame, polarising, which is when you see everything as either black or white with no grey, and catastrophizing, which is when you prepare for the worst, are examples of common forms of this. These cognitive processes are all useless.

Throughout the entire week, pay attention to your reactions and inner dialogue. Stop yourself if you see any of these actions happening. Avoid self-criticism and strive to appreciate and accept oneself instead. The better you are with yourself, the happier the people and circumstances in your life will make you.

When you notice yourself thinking negatively, change to a more positive and constructive attitude. Keep your self-talk to things you wouldn't dare say to others. Consider yourself like you would a child or a grandparent, and treat yourself with kindness and inspiration. Here are a few instances:

Use Affirmations: Although they may come off as cheesy, affirmations are actually quite effective at encouraging a positive outlook. Affirmations can help you eliminate negative ideas and rewire your brain to think more positively. Use affirmations seriously and with intention. The effectiveness of affirmations is a topic that is covered in a lot of literature. Take ideas from these books and use the list in the Tools and Resources section of this book to compose your own affirmations. Read them in the morning and at night. When you need motivation, read these aloud to yourself.

Have a sense of humour: Try to find the funny side of events that don't go as planned. Laugh at yourself, especially in hard circumstances. You can relieve tension and stress from unfavourable situations by laughing. Spending time with those who can laugh even in the most awkward situations is also valued. To avoid contributing to negativity, try not to take yourself too seriously. Keep your spirits up and try to find the funny in even the worst situations.

Take Care of Yourself: Taking steps to maintain your physical and mental health will help you on the path to a healthy self-image. By itself, this will promote self-assurance and reduce self-critical thoughts. Exercise also produces hormones that improve mood, make you feel good, and lower stress.

Create Healthy Relationships: Surround yourself with positive people and avoid negative people. Create a network of people you can turn to for support and assistance. Reduce the amount of time you spend with negative people if you want to minimise the negativity in your life. Even if they are a friend or relative, you don't have to fully cut them out of your life; you only need to set limits and maintain the proper distance.

Encourage an attitude of gratitude by setting aside some time each day to reflect on all the blessings in your life. Be thankful for both yourself and other people. Never-good-enough thinking could come across negatively and turn people off. But expressing gratitude enhances your charm and attracts good vibes to you.

Let Go: Release things outside of your scope of control. It's okay that sometimes you won't be able to change how other people behave or how the situation is. Worrying about things you can't change simply makes you more anxious and negative. When you see that you are becoming dependent on anything, stop and consider whether it is truly necessary to invest so much negative energy in it.

Celebrate Your Successes and Strengths: Everyone possesses their own unique strengths and has achieved a number of noteworthy life goals. Don't forget to thank them repeatedly. List your accomplishments and strengths in the corresponding sections of the List of Strengths and List of Accomplishments, which may be found under Tools and Resources in Part III. If you run out of space, use a notebook or notepad to compile a list. Keep the list nearby at all times so you can refer to it frequently. Reviewing these lists frequently will help you adopt a happier outlook on life.

Ignore Your Fears: Negativity thrives on fear and anxiety. Many people allow their fears of the future to prevent them from moving forward, from having hope, or from achieving the objectives that will make their lives enjoyable. Be open to possibilities and set aside your fear of the unknown.

Apply the Law of Attraction. The law of attraction has existed for centuries, despite its current rise in popularity. Simply said, it asks you to focus on what you want and what you want to attract into your life rather than the negative, annoying, or disappointing things. When we dwell on the bad, we become motionless and run out of energy. However, focusing on what you desire makes it easier for you to see positive outcomes and inspires you to take action to make them a reality.

Extra Points

Already an upbeat person? You can go a step further by encouraging those who are close to you to adopt a more upbeat outlook. If you surround yourself with positive people more frequently, your life will be filled with more positive energy and you'll be happier.

Every Day, Take A Multivitamin

We occasionally eat properly and occasionally not. All the vitamins, minerals, and other nutrients required for optimum health and regular operation are only sometimes obtained by humans. The greatest method to ensure that you consume enough food, particularly plant-based foods, is to eat healthy. However, it could be challenging to continuously consume the daily recommended doses of each vitamin in practice.

Even though it isn't always a good idea to take every supplement available, taking a multivitamin is a prudent course of action. As an insurance policy for a balanced diet, think about it. No matter what, it guarantees that you consume the recommended daily intake of the nutrients you require. While this does not absolve you from eating healthily or being mindful of what you put in your body, it does ensure that it receives the nutrients it needs despite challenges like travel, hurried lunch breaks, busy schedules, and other challenges life may throw your way.

Despite the fact that taking vitamins may seem like a safer option to improve your nutrition, doing so can be dangerous. As an illustration, taking vitamin A, C, E, or any other antioxidant vitamin alone may have a pro-oxidative effect and significantly reduce the effectiveness of antioxidant defences. In contrast, multivitamins are made so that the vitamins and minerals work together to provide the greatest amount of health advantages.

.

An Approach To Success

Look for multivitamins that don't contain more vitamins or minerals than the daily recommended intakes (DRI) to prevent taking too much of a particular nutrient.

Food products are governed by FDA regulations before they are sold, and supplements are also subject to their examination after they are available for purchase. Additionally, before creating and distributing supplements, supplement makers are not required to register their products with the FDA or obtain their approval. So, always go with a multivitamin made by a reputable, well-known company.

Before taking any supplements, talk to your doctor if you have any health issues, are pregnant, or are nursing a child.

Extra Points

Already taking a multivitamin every day? Probiotics should also be considered. Our intestines need to be home to healthy bacteria for digestion to occur. If you don't regularly eat items that have undergone fermentation, such as yoghurt, you could not be getting enough healthy bacteria for healthy digestion.

As a result, you might think about including probiotics as a nutritional supplement in your diet. Probiotics improve digestion by maintaining a healthy balance of the good bacteria in our intestines.

Be aware that some yoghourts of lower quality might not actually contain as many beneficial bacteria as other yoghurt types. Look for yoghourts that are all-natural, pure, and free of additives.

Keep Strangers At A Distance

Our health and overall level of comfort in daily life can be greatly impacted by the air we breathe. Our lungs, eyes, and noses can be harmed by pollutants, allergies, and toxins, which can leave us feeling less than our best. Every time we enter our homes, we bring a ton of poisonous substances with us on our shoes, clothing, and other belongings. Dust, pollen, mildew, and filth are some of the most hazardous substances that can enter from the outside during extreme weather, along with water, snow, ice, and muck.

In order to maintain clean and healthy air inside your home, you must construct a space or a buffer zone where you can take off your shoes and enter from the outside. There will be fewer incidences of asthma and allergies, better indoor air quality, fewer harmful chemicals, and, in some situations, increased energy efficiency. And lastly, it will make cleaning the house much easier!

The News, I Hear

Hay fever, the sixth most common chronic condition in people, is a major contributor to "presenteeism," or neglecting to show up for work. It accounts for over four million absences annually and costs more than $700 million in lost productivity.

The Shift

To reduce the quantity of unpleasant external toxins that enter your home, take off your shoes at the door and designate a transition area.

An Approach To Success

Follow these recommendations to avoid leaving outdoor contaminants behind:

blankets and socks Establish a "no shoes" policy for visitors as well when they enter your home. Remove your shoes as soon as you arrive at your home. Wear socks or indoor slippers indoors, or go barefoot outside. You could even wish to give each visitor a pair of warm slippers or socks. As a result, your home will be significantly less exposed to debris, pollen, dust, and other contaminants.

Locate the region that will profit from a buffer. The most popular entrance to your home would be the best location. All utility rooms, garage, and other common area entrances and exits should have buffer zones.

Flooring: A hard surface that is simple to maintain, especially water resistant, and doesn't gather dust or other debris makes for the greatest flooring for your transition zone. If your entrance does not currently have flooring, you might want to consider installing some (with a surface area of around 5' by 5'). Additional details about appropriate flooring are available under Extra Credit.

Accessories: Whether or whether your buffer zone has a hard surface, you should utilise the following accessories to reduce the quantity of dirt and other undesired pollutants that enter your home: A shoe scraper can be used to remove the majority of the snow and ice from the area outside your entryway.

Outside Mat: You could wish to lay out an outdoor mat and a shoe scraper for visitors to use before entering the property.

There should be a tiny, non-skid area rug at the entrance to your buffer zone that can gather dirt, wetness, and dust from shoes. This is true whether your flooring is hard or entirely carpeted.

Provide a rubber, waterproof shoe tray or mat in your transition area so that shoes can dry properly by dripping on it. To keep water off your floor, use one that can retain and catch any that your shoes may drop.

Even if a bench is not strictly necessary, it will be more convenient for individuals to take off their soiled shoes. In order to swiftly put on your slippers or socks at the door, look for a bench with storage.

Once more, this is not required, but if you live in a humid area, an exhaust fan can assist with sufficient ventilation to prevent the growth of mildew or mould due to standing water. It also hastens the drying of drenched garments and footwear.

Hooks and baskets If you don't have a coat closet, hang bags and jackets on the hooks you built in your transition area at the entryway. To prevent umbrellas from dripping water onto your floors, install an umbrella holder or container there.

The News, I Hear

More than 50% of homes, according to a recent survey, have at least six allergies that are readily apparent.

Extra Points

By creating a transition area and removing your shoes at the door, are you already putting the outdoors behind you? Add another airtight transition door (double door entrance) to an existing mudroom if you have the area; typical sizes range from 6' x 6' to 7' x 9'. You might be able to accomplish this in order to keep pollutants outside, lower your energy expenditures, and lessen the amount of severely hot or cold air that enters your home.

Excellent mudroom surfaces include ceramic tile and stone flooring. Tiles are moisture-resistant, hygienic, and aesthetically pleasing. Use darker grout colours since they tend to cover dirt better and make sure the grout is non-slip.

Concrete: When coloured or etched, concrete can be a gorgeous replacement for tile or stone. Additionally, cleaning it is easy.

Floor made of bamboo Moisture and dirt have the potential to harm hardwood flooring. But the surface of bamboo flooring is much stronger and resistant to damage. Not only is it fantastic and lovely, but it is also environmentally beneficial. For best energy efficiency, if you have pets, install pet doors on the exterior door.

Take Some Vegetables

Thank you for visiting the Holy Cabbage Church. Take some lettuce, please. Mom was right to insist that we eat our vegetables, unknown author. Vegetables are nutrient-dense superstars for sustaining optimum health. They include an abundance of phytonutrients, fibre, vitamins, and minerals that delay the onset of disease, obesity, and ageing. Vegetables are a good source of potassium, folate, vitamin A, vitamin E, and vitamin C, among other nutrients.

Due to their high water content and extremely low calorie and fat contents, fibrous vegetables (peppers, carrots, and leafy greens) are especially helpful for weight loss since they make you feel satisfied on a relatively low calorie diet. They also have a high fibre content, which aids in good digestion, reduces the risk of heart disease, and brings down blood cholesterol levels.

Because they contain so many phytonutrients, vegetables have brilliant colours. The phytonutrients present in plants are thought to have positive effects on health. Even while veggies come in a variety of colours and include a variety of other nutrients, eating vegetables of all hues of the rainbow helps to ensure that you are getting a wide variety of nutrients that safeguard your health in your diet. The book Every Color of the Rainbow—Vegetables explores the phytonutrients and health benefits associated with common vegetables, as well as their hues:

The Change

Eat at least four to six servings of fibre-rich vegetables each day. One serving is equal to either 1 cup of leafy vegetables or 1/2 cup of non-leafy vegetables.

A Strategy For Success

Including vegetables in your diet, whether you like them or not, is crucial for leading a healthy lifestyle. Here are some tips:

Start with those you find appealing: If you don't typically eat a lot of vegetables, you can develop the misconception that you don't enjoy them. Instead than focusing on the things you dislike, consider the things you value. Look at the fruit in all of its varied colours that is depicted on the chart. Focus this week on consuming four to six servings of the meals you are confident you will love.

Investigate a different veggie each week. To learn how to prepare unusual vegetables, look out recipes online. All three of these websites—www.cookinglight.com, www.sparkrecipes.com, and www.eatingwell.com—offer healthy recipe options.

Prepare for the upcoming week by: To ensure that you obtain the proper serving sizes when you eat at home, make sure to include enough veggies in your dishes when planning your meals for the week. If you are cooking for more than just yourself, be sure to triple the amounts per person. Make a note of all the vegetables you want to buy and, whenever possible, choose to buy seasonal, fresh food because it will taste the best.

Find Alternatives When Necessary: If fresh vegetables aren't an option, go with frozen. Vegetables that are frozen are frequently quickly frozen and don't have a lot of additives, like sodium or salt. Canned vegetables should be avoided, though, as they frequently include additives and preservatives. The only exception to this rule is tomato cans. Only tomatoes come in cans and have as many benefits. In fact, due to their higher concentration, stewed tomatoes, crushed tomatoes, and tomato sauces may contain more lycopene than fresh tomatoes. Consume only tomato-based foods that also contain seasonings and other ingredients; look for foods without added sugar.

Make Wise Breakfast Choices: Make the healthy switch from starchy potatoes, which are typically eaten as a vegetable for breakfast, to fibre-rich vegetables. Add a few handfuls of baby spinach or chopped peppers, onions, mushrooms, asparagus, or tomatoes to omelettes, frittatas, or eggs. If you want to cut back on the amount of needless oil and carbohydrates, choose sliced fresh tomato as a side dish rather than home fries.

Lunch and dinner salads One of the simplest methods to increase your intake of vegetables is to make a large, colourful salad the first meal of every lunch and dinner. Grill some chicken breast, shrimp, or fish for your main course and add it to a salad. You can add as many vegetables to your salad as you wish, including carrots, celery, cucumbers, peppers, onions, tomatoes, mushrooms, and broccoli.

Another excellent option is dark leafy greens like spinach, arugula, or baby romaine. Get pre washed greens in bags if you don't have much time, and then prepare the salad ingredients for the following week. Vegetables that have been sliced up should be stored in containers in the refrigerator for quick and easy salad preparation. You can include fruit, such as apples, pears, and grapes, to make salads a little tastier.

Use salad dressings sparingly to lower your intake of sugar and fat. Use extra virgin olive oil, other monounsaturated-fat-rich oils (such canola, peanut, or sesame oil), vinegar, mustard, and spices to make your own dressing when it is practical. When using a prepared or packaged dressing, vinaigrettes are preferred to those made with cream or mayonnaise.

Develop Sides If salad isn't your entree, start the night with a salad and serve your main course with a side (or two) of vegetables. For a quick, low-fat side dish, vegetables can be steamed, broiler roasted, grilled, or baked. After being cooked, cauliflower, broccoli, Brussels sprouts, carrots, green beans, and asparagus all maintain their unique flavours. Sautéing spinach, kale, and collard greens in a mixture of olive oil, garlic, and lemon also tastes nice. If you prefer raw vegetables over cooked ones, serve a cup of them as a side dish.

Sandwiches: Add more vegetables to your sandwiches for a hearty and full evening. Along with lettuce and tomatoes, other sliced vegetables that can be added for more nutrition include pepper, cucumber, onion, mushrooms, and carrots. Make vegetable wraps with cucumbers, roasted peppers, lettuce, and onions for an extra protein boost. Serve them with plain, nonfat Greek yoghurt or hummus.

Onions and peppers are excellent additions to casseroles, sauces, meatloaf, chilli, and stews, along with other veggies including squash, carrots, eggplant, zucchini, and broccoli. To test if you appreciate a new vegetable, incorporate it into several of your dishes.

sliced vegetables as a snack For quick and easy snacks, vegetables can be cut up and stored in Ziploc bags or other containers. Broccoli, peppers, carrots, celery, cherry tomatoes, and other crunchy veggies make delectable nibbles.

Simple to Combine For a full, nutrient-dense snack when you're short on time, think about mixing a handful of these ingredients:

1. 1 cup of carrots and 1/4 cup of hummus
2. 1 cup of celery sticks and 1 ounce of low-fat cheese
3. 1 cup of cucumbers with garlic and dill and 1/2 cup of nonfat Greek yoghurt.

Starchy Versus Fibrous Vegetables

Even though starchy foods like corn and potatoes offer healthy nutrients, they digest more quickly than fibrous vegetables and have a higher calorie density. You should cut back on your consumption and focus on consuming more fibre-rich vegetables.

Exists Extra Credit already? You can make significant progress if you concentrate on the variety of vegetables you consume. Make sure you consume at least one serving of vegetables from every colour of the rainbow every day or every other day. As a result, food will include the largest amount of phytonutrients, vitamins, and minerals that fight disease.

Additionally, nutritionally speaking, vegetables with darker colours are substantially richer than those with lighter colours. For example, spinach is more nutrient-dense than iceberg lettuce. Some vegetables that are rich in nutrients include broccoli, orange and red peppers, tomatoes, dark leafy greens (like spinach and kale), mixed greens, carrots, red cabbage, eggplant, and zucchini. Other members of the lily family, including asparagus, chives, onions, garlic, leeks, and shallots, also have compounds that contain sulphur and may be protective against cancer.

Enjoy Your Solitude

Life is busy. We feel as though there is no time left for the "want tos" because our days are so full of "have tos." Furthermore, we lose the ability to recharge and unwind when we spend all of our time with other people. Lack of time can result in uncontrolled stress, annoyance, fatigue, resentment, or even worse, health problems. Additionally, it could keep us from doing the things we enjoy or who we are. Routine "you time" scheduling, however, offers a lot of advantages that all combine to make life a little bit sweeter and more tolerable.

You have the opportunity to consider the characteristics that make you who you are while you are alone yourself. You can enjoy hobbies, discover new passions, rekindle old ones, and make objectives to build the life you want when you have some alone time. Unfortunately, a lot of people find it difficult to succeed because they are unable to put their own needs before those of others.

However, spending time alone encourages you to take a break from routine obligations and other people's expectations so that you can set aside time to develop with your own objectives, attend to your own needs, and further explore your particular aspirations. It assists in breaking up the monotony so that you can enjoy life and have a zest for life.

You can decompress and organise the day's chaos when you get some alone time, which helps you see things from a new angle. Being able to think clearly enables you to focus on what matters most to you without the interference of outside factors. You are able to be more decisive and establish ideas based just on your thoughts because of the absence of outside influences.

Even while being alone can be tough and uncomfortable for many people, overcoming the discomfort can promote independence and self-confidence. As a result, you gain more independence, which makes it simpler for you to trust your judgement and the decisions you make. You'll quickly experience a sense of empowerment that will allow you to live a better life and make wiser decisions.

And finally, you can manage your stress better when you're alone. It enables you to step back, unwind, and release some of the pressure and tension you encounter every day. Your physical and emotional health are both impacted by your capacity to handle daily stress.

The Shift

Every day, set aside at least 30 minutes for yourself.

An approach to success

It can seem excessive to set aside 30 to 60 minutes each day for yourself, but consider this: One hour is about equal to one-fourth of your complete day in the big picture. Plan ahead and, more importantly, give yourself first priority. Here are a few ideas:

Accept It In: Get out of bed 30 minutes earlier or stay in bed 30 minutes later each day this week. Of course, you should make an effort to keep to a regular seven to eight hour sleep pattern. Consider adjusting the rest of the day if you don't have much time. For instance, if you work, spend your lunch break working alone on something significant to you. Make arrangements for someone to watch your children for an hour if you work from home or are a stay-at-home mom. Use your imagination to identify and set aside some time exclusively for you while keeping an eye out for choices that are already feasible.

Organise a meeting If you have a calendar, make sure to block off time for yourself so it feels like an appointment. The likelihood that something or someone will eat it will be reduced because this will stop it from opening up.

Put technology beyond reach: After eight o'clock at night, turn off your laptop, phone, and any other distracting technology. To give your eyes and mind a rest from the continual distractions, turn off technology until a certain time in the morning. Timetables for children's activities If you have kids, give their routines more rigidity so you can spend more time on your own.

Steps to Take

The time you set aside for yourself might not be used as you intended. Despite the fact that I've listed a few possibilities below, the most crucial thing is that you do something you enjoy. Keep in mind that this is your time, so taking advantage of it whatsoever makes you feel most satisfied.

Exercise: If you plan to spend some time alone in the morning, take use of the opportunity. Go for a walk, visit the gym, or register for a yoga class. You can wake up with the aid of these exercises and get ready for the day. If it's tough for you to get to the gym, invest in some home exercise equipment so you can exercise comfortably and easily.

Read: Reading is a great way to spend time alone while also escaping a little from your own life, whether you want to catch up on the latest news or want to dive into a new romance.

Connection to Nature: Spending time in nature can help you find inspiration, unleash your creativity, and rediscover your inner self. Take a deep breath, notice how beautiful your surroundings are, and listen to the sounds of nature to quiet your mind.

Attend a lecture, a lesson, or a documentary to learn. Find a new passion or activity that you can engage in occasionally or regularly for enjoyment.

Explore a new part of your town or neighbourhood on foot, by car, bicycle, or rollerblades.

To broaden your cultural awareness, attend plays, concerts, movies, theatrical productions, concerts, or museums. Immerse yourself in cultural activities and performances to broaden your horizons.

Take on a Project: Have you given organising your closets any thought? Have you considered undertaking a home improvement project? Spend some alone time starting and finishing the tasks you've been putting off.

Get treated: Spend an hour getting a facial or massage. Get your nails and feet done. Don't allow guilt to prevent you from giving yourself some alone time. Take it in!

Extra Points

Already scheduled at least 30 minutes per day for solitude? To obtain a few additional hours of solitude, schedule weekly dates with yourself. Visit a spa, go hiking, or take a road trip. Engage in enjoyable, uplifting, and joyous activities.

Stretching That Takes A Long Time

Exercises like aerobics or strength training are frequently associated with being physically fit. Typically, stretching or flexibility training comes last. Stretching can actually assist people in achieving a higher level of fitness over the course of their lives, but many people are unaware of this.

We must contract and flex our muscles during strength training and aerobic exercise. Our muscles naturally tighten as we get older, and our range of motion gradually declines. We are more vulnerable to harm as a result. But stretching improves our all-day flexibility and productivity. As a result, we are less likely to get hurt and can live more active lives.

Stretching is necessary for stress management and decrease. We frequently hold the most tension in the muscles across our entire body. While some individuals may have neck stiffness, others may harbour stress in their lower backs. Wherever stress may be present, stretching helps with muscular relaxation and tension release. By improving blood flow to the muscles, it also enhances circulation, boosting energy levels and accelerating muscle recovery.

The Shift

Maintain flexibility by stretching for at least 20 minutes three times each week.

An Approach To Success

It doesn't take a lot of time or expensive equipment to stretch. It's also possible everywhere. Before starting any stretching or exercising routine, be sure to check with your doctor or physical therapist if you have any chronic illnesses or injuries.

A Splash of Growth

Stretching is advised anytime, everywhere, but it's crucial before and after exertion. After a warm-up and after a cool-down, stretch. Your muscles are now warmed up, making stretching simpler and more efficient.

Take a quick five-minute stroll while pumping your arms to stimulate blood flow to warm up your muscles before stretching outside of activities. Stretch that part of your body more regularly or continuously throughout the day if it is particularly stiff.

Vehicle Laws

Keep the following in mind when stretching safely and effectively: Hold each stretch for ten to thirty seconds after performing it two to four times.

Always begin stretching with the legs, back, and chest, then move on to the shoulders, biceps, and triceps.

Set boundaries: Stretching should result in a little, transient strain or discomfort; however, if you experience severe pain, you've gone too far. If you feel any discomfort, gradually lessen the stretch until it passes. From the area where pain is no longer experienced, begin the stretch. To avoid overusing or damaging the other muscles, try to keep them apart by concentrating on just one at a time.

Don't bounce: The safest method to develop flexibility is static stretching, which is slowly extending a muscle through its complete range of motion until resistance is felt and holding the stretch for ten to thirty seconds. Although bouncing while stretching was fashionable a few decades ago, doing so may cause minor muscular tears that can result in scar tissue, tighter muscles, and injury. Therefore, to avoid injury, just conduct static stretching.

Breathe: While stretching, make sure to take calm, deep breaths. Be patient, breathe deeply throughout the stretch, and don't rush because muscles require some time to lengthen, especially if they are tight.

Some Stretching Ideas

There are stretching courses and other programs involving some stretching at the majority of gyms and fitness facilities. Enrolling in a class could be a wonderful method to learn about common stretches if you're new to stretching.

Stretching can be incorporated into your everyday life in many different ways, including yoga and pilates. You may get a well-rounded exercise by including flexibility, deep breathing, and strength training into many yoga and Pilates practices. They also encourage longer stretches, which have been shown to increase flexibility, range of motion, and general wellness in many students.

Exercising Flexibility

There are several stretches you can perform on your own or at home. The stretches that follow, however, are straightforward and concentrate on all significant muscle groups. Unless otherwise specified, hold each stretch for at least ten seconds.

Your knees should be slightly bent as you stand with your feet shoulder width apart. Bring your hands to your chest and clench them together in front of you. Pull your hands slowly away from your body as if you were carrying a beach ball while you look down toward the ground. To feel the stretch in your upper back, look for a small gap between your shoulder blades. Stretching of the upper back is depicted in figure.

Standing with your feet shoulder-width apart, knees slightly bent, and arms at your sides, perform the upper back stretch. Join your hands and extend both of your arms behind you. To feel a stretch in your chest and shoulders, clasp your hands behind your back and bring them toward the floor. As high and back as your joined hands will allow you to comfortably support yourself.

If you are unable to clasp your hands behind your back, you have two choices: You can either hold a strap, belt, or scarf behind your back with both hands as tightly as you can without putting undue strain on the joints, or rest your hands on your lower back and squeeze your elbows together to feel a stretch in your chest. While slowly raising them as high as they will go or until you feel the stretch, keep your arms as straight as you can. Stretch out your chest.

Tightness In The Chest

A chair will be placed by your right side as you stand to exercise your quads. Bend your left leg so that your foot is facing up toward your buttocks while holding the chair with your right hand. It is appropriate to hold your left ankle with your left hand. Standing straight, bring your left foot gently into your buttocks to lengthen the stretch. Once you're done, repeat on the opposite side.

Working out your quadriceps Lay down on the ground to work your hamstrings. Your legs should be bent and your feet should be flat on the ground. Lift your right leg up vertically toward the ceiling. Slowly tuck your right leg into your chest while placing both hands on your right thigh. Maximise leg straightness while avoiding knee locking. Take ten seconds to hold. Hamstring stretches are shown in the figure. Repeat on the other side after releasing.

Stretching the lower back and hamstrings You should sit on the floor with your hands and knees together. Your knees should be directly behind your hips and your wrists should be in line with your shoulders. Tuck your toes under and pull your chest away from your abdomen as you inhale. Your tailbone ought to be facing up.

During this stretch, be cautious to lift your attention to the ceiling. A lower back stretch is shown in Figure 1. The tops of your feet should be resting on the floor as you return to a neutral position. Elevate your lower back like a cat, point your belly button in the direction of your spine, and turn your head so you are looking back at your legs as you exhale. Figure 2 shows a total of six stretches for the lower back.

Lower Back Stretch

Stretching the lower back twice Calves: Place a chair or a wall an arm's length away from you. Leaning forward, position your hands shoulder-width apart on the chair back or the wall. Step backwards with your right foot while keeping your left foot firmly on the ground. Until you feel a stretch in your right leg, lean your hips and body toward the chair or wall. Take another step back with your foot to stretch more deeply. Once you're done, repeat on the opposite side.

Standing with your feet shoulder-width apart and your knees slightly bent is the ideal position for performing the calf stretch. Make sure your right arm is crossed across your torso and parallel to the ground. Place your left hand over your right arm and gently press it into your body without moving your torso. Think about the illustration's shoulder extension. Once you're done, repeat on the opposite side.

Shoulders Elongated

Standing with your feet shoulder width apart, your knees should be slightly bent. You tilt your head downward and scan the surface. Till you get a stretch in the back of your neck, gently push the back of your head with both of your hands. The back of the neck should be stretched.

Figure: Extending The Neck's Back

Your right ear should be next to your right shoulder as you maintain your forward look while angling your head to the right. Gently press with your right hand on the left side of your head until you feel a stretch in the left side of your neck. Once you're done, repeat on the opposite side.

Stretching on one side of the neck To exercise your biceps, stand with your feet shoulder-width apart and slightly bent knees. Set your arms shoulder-height apart and straight out to the side. Turn your wrists so that your hands' backs are facing up. Consider the illustration's biceps stretch.

Stretch your triceps and biceps. Your knees should be slightly bent as you stand with your feet shoulder width apart. your right arm is raised high. Your right arm should be bent such that your elbow is straight up and facing your spine. To enlarge your triceps, use your left hand to gently press on the outside of your elbow. Your triceps should be stretched as in Figure. Once you're done, repeat on the opposite side.

Triceps Extension Bonus Point

Already extremely flexible? By including stretching in your daily routine, you may maintain blood flow and energy levels in addition to exercising.

Early Every Day: Muscles frequently become tight from inactivity while we sleep. Gentle morning stretches may assist to reduce stiffness and promote circulation, which makes waking up easier even though it's better to stretch when your muscles are warm. To avoid straining yourself, be sure to start stretching slowly.

Following a Long Sitting Period: Muscles can get extremely tight and uncomfortable when seated for long periods of time, whether at work, on an airline, or when watching TV. You should stand up, walk around, and perform some of the stretches mentioned above no later than an hour.

Check the Box

You can tell how healthy (or hazardous) a packaged food or product is just by reading the Ingredient List and Nutrition Facts panel. You will have the knowledge and power to make better informed food decisions once you learn how to read these labels.

Making healthier decisions will be made easier if you know how to read the Nutrition Facts and Ingredients panels on packaged goods.

An Approach To Success

Since each provides a distinct kind of information, the Ingredient List and the Nutrition Facts panel should be used in tandem. When combined, they offer a window into the food's quality, the quality of its components, and the balance of its nutrients.

Have you heard of it?

A poll found that almost 40% of Americans never look at the Nutrition Facts panel before purchasing food. The study was published in the American Dietetic Association Journal. In addition, 56% of individuals don't even glance at the health claims, and 50% of people don't even read the ingredient list.

Getting Going

Take some packaged food from your cabinets. As you learn to read labels, use these as examples. Consider the product's healthfulness while you read the extensive details of the Ingredient List and the Nutrition Facts panel. To keep on track, use the Nutrition Label Analysis—Worksheet, which can be found in the Tools and Resources area.

The list of Ingredients

The ingredients, spices, and possibly-used chemicals that are utilised to prepare the cuisine are all listed in the ingredient list. Beginning with the heaviest ingredient—which comprises the majority of the food—and moving down the list in order of decreasing weight is the lightest ingredient—which comprises the smallest portion of the dish. In essence, the Ingredient List provides you a sense of the product's ingredient quality.

Anything containing any of the following should be avoided:

1. Bleached, unbleached, or refined flours
2. Processed foods that aren't organic or whole
3. Ingredients you find challenging to pronounce, have never heard of, or contain the word "artificial"
4. More than five ingredients on a very long list
5. The first three ingredients on the list should be added fat, oils, and sugar (or any of its derivatives).
6. Remember that extra fats and carbs might have a wide variety of shapes and names.
7. Sugar Forms We Know
8. Liquid from the agave
9. Juice with dark sugar crystals
10. Maple syrup
11. Grain syrup or sweetener derived from fructose crystals found in corn
12. Juice produced with dextrose from cane vapour
13. Juice concentrates sweetened with glucose and fructose corn syrup
14. Inverted Maltose sugar with honey Milk sugar molasses syrup
15. Unrefined molasses sugar
16. Sucrose-sweetened syrup
17. Turbinado
18. known to exist as fats
19. Butter, cream, and coconut oil are all hydrophobic oils and diglycerides of lard from palm kernel oil Shortening made in part from palm oil and hydrogenated oils

Board for Food and Nutrition

To help us make the healthiest decisions, the Nutrition Facts panel offers a thorough analysis of the nutritional content of packaged foods and products. In essence, they give us detailed information on how various things compare to one another. See the Nutrition Facts panel below for a complete explanation of this panel.

The Panel's Upper Half

The Nutrition Facts panel's most significant section is this one. This information can be used to evaluate a food product's nutritional worth.

The size of a serving. The serving size includes a recommendation for serving size. Measure or weigh your servings if you are unsure. Be aware that the remaining information on the panel needs to be changed if you consume more or less than the recommended portion size. For instance, if you eat double the serving, all nutritional values must be multiplied by two. Last but not least, while assessing food products, compare serving sizes that are equal.

Calories taken in. You eat the amount of calories that each serving of food offers in terms of energy. Keep in mind that if you eat something in two servings, you will consume double the amount of calories. If a serving of a food has 100 calories or fewer, it is considered to be relatively low in calories; if it has more than 350 calories, it is considered to be relatively high in calories.

Fat-derived calories. This lists the calories and fat content of each suggested serving. An average of nine calories are present in every gram of fat. Typically, 20 to 30 percent of your daily calories should come from fat. You should limit your intake of fat to 30 calories per 100 calories of food as a result.

The composition of all fat. Less unhealthy fat and more healthy fat should be consumed, in that order. You can identify the different types of fats present in different foods by using the information provided here.

In general, fat. The amount of good (mono- and polyunsaturated) and bad (saturated and trans) fats in a food can be determined by looking at the total amount of fat in that food. This amount of fat per 100 calories should not be more than 3 grams in order to stay within the 20 to 30% range.

Unhealthy fats, b. In general, saturated fats are unhealthy. They can be found in whole milk, eggs, palm and coconut oils, butter, margarine, meat, poultry, and pork fats, as well as many fast foods. It is advisable to avoid or consume foods high in saturated fat to a very small amount. Limit your intake to one gram every 100 calories.

The trans fats, c. Trans fats are produced during food processing and are frequently found in professionally made baked goods. You should stop consuming these, and search for goods whose Nutrition Facts panel lists 0 grams of these.

Unfortunately, information on the ratio of polyunsaturated and monounsaturated fat is not always included on Nutrition Facts panels. In these cases, comparing the amounts of saturated and trans fat to the total amount of fat is the most accurate way to assess whether the product contains any of these fats. There are extremely few, if any, beneficial fats in the product if the values are equal to or nearly equal to the total amount of fat in grams. So it's advisable to stay away from the food.

Triglycerides and sodium. Always choose the packaged food with the lowest salt and cholesterol levels per serving when comparing similar-sized servings of different foods.

Cholesterol is A. The FDA recommends not taking more than 300 milligrams of cholesterol daily. Dietary cholesterol has been the subject of recent debate. Dietary cholesterol may not be a severe problem, even while blood cholesterol is. According to a study, the quantity of cholesterol absorbed by diet and the amount measured in the blood are only tangentially related.

The quantity of cholesterol that is absorbed during meals has a negligibly little effect on the blood cholesterol levels of many persons. On some people, though, it might have a significant impact. Therefore, it may be wise to reduce your intake of cholesterol from food sources if you have high cholesterol or a family history of high cholesterol. If you'd like more information on this subject, speak with your doctor.

Sweetener b. It is well known that consuming too much sodium can harm your health. You should limit your intake to 2,300 mg per day at most.

Carbohydrate disintegration. You should consume more complex and high-fibre foods and fewer items made from sugar or other processed foods when it comes to carbohydrates.

Every carbohydrate. Sugars, complex carbs, and fibre are all included in the total amount of carbohydrates. On average, four calories are present in every gram of carbohydrate. Carbohydrates should make up 40–60% of your total calories, or 10-15 grams for every 100 calories, in a healthy diet.

Food fibre, b. A healthy diet must include fibre as a key component. It is present in the majority of plant-based foods, such as whole grains, fruits, vegetables, legumes, and beans. It is recommended to ingest 25 to 35 grams of fibre per day, or 2 grams for every 100 calories.

Sugars; c. You want to see as little sugar on the Nutrition Facts screen as possible. Maximum daily added sugar intakes range from 32 to 36 grams. Natural sugar present in entire fruits and dairy products is not considered "added sugar" and is instead referred to as such.

Lean meat: In general, it's best to maintain a consistent balance of protein, carbohydrates, and fats in meals and snacks. If a food has a low protein level, pair it with another protein-rich item to make a well-rounded snack or meal. Protein has a calorie content of about four per gram, similar to carbs. You should get 20 to 40 percent of your calories, or 5 to 10 grams of protein per 100 calories, from protein.

Ratios for every day. The amount that a serving adds to the suggested daily intake of fat, cholesterol, salt, carbs, and fibre is shown in the Daily Values section. These proportions are based on a diet of 2,000 calories. A percentage of 20% is seen as high, and one of 5% as low. Because they could alter if you consume more or fewer than 2,000 calories per day, these percentages should only be used as a general guide.

The Panel's Lower Half

This information won't be very useful to the great majority of consumers. A 2,000 calorie diet is the basis of the majority of it. Additionally, the data is lacking and ought to only be used as a guide. As a result, each part is given merely a brief summary.

Minerals and vitamins. These figures show how many of a few specific vitamins and minerals are needed in a serving of the food product each day. Take a daily multivitamin, as instructed in week six, to make sure you are getting all the vitamins and minerals you need each day.

The doses that are advised. The total recommended daily intake for each nutrient is given for diets of 2,000 calories and 2,500 calories. If you need to eat more or less than 2,000 or 2,500 calories per day to maintain a healthy body weight, the recommended intakes for fat, cholesterol, sodium, and carbohydrates will change.

Calories per gram, or 11. There are various calorie counts per gram of fat, carbohydrate, and protein, as was already mentioned. You are reminded of the caloric weight of each food item in this section of the label.

Nutrition Facts Panel Synopsis

The following chart gives you a summary of the caloric weight of each nutrient (when applicable), the number of grams of each nutrient you should include in your diet, and the overall percentage of calories that should be devoted to the nutrient (when applicable). This will help you understand some of the specifics covered this week. This can be used as a quick reference guide while examining packaged food products.

Place it in the Square Public

Go to the shop and check prices on some of the things you buy most regularly after you can read these labels. Compare this to items like yoghurt, bread, pasta sauces, and anything else you routinely purchase. Start paying attention to the contents in food products as well as their nutritional makeup and balance so that you may pick healthier options.

Deepen Your Breath

Breathing is usually taken for granted; we do it without thinking or conscious effort. However, deep, focused breathing is a straightforward movement with enormous potential. It can improve digestion, decrease blood pressure, and calm stress.

Typically, most people breathe from their chest. Stress also makes us breathe more fast, which lowers the amount of oxygen we can take in and increases our levels of tension and anxiety. In addition to your lungs, deep breathing also allows you to breathe into your abdomen or diaphragm. Your brain receives a signal when these deeper muscles are engaged urging it to relax and calm down. Your heart rate, breathing rate, and blood pressure eventually decrease as a result of your body receiving that signal.

We utilise our neck and shoulders to lift our rib cage and expand our chest when we don't breathe deeply, which makes us more prone to tension headaches. Deep breathing, on the other hand, keeps these muscles loose and prevents the development of unwelcome tension and rigidity.

Finally, deep breathing relaxes our internal organs because it works our diaphragm and abdominal muscles. This could promote regularity and improve digestion as a result.

Spend five to ten minutes each day deep breathing.

An Approach To Success

Deep breathing may be practised anytime, anywhere, and is not just a really simple modification to make. There are many methods to do it, but the following offers a straightforward, step-by-step tutorial for fundamental deep breathing:

1. Make sure your back is straight and find a comfy seat. Cross-legged seating is a common posture.
2. Grasp your tummy with one hand and your chest with the other.
3. Inhale deeply through your nose. While the hand on your chest should barely move at all, the hand on your stomach should rise.

By tightening your abdominal muscles and bringing your belly button closer to your spine, exhale as much air as you can through your lips. When you exhale, the hand that is resting on your stomach should move in, but the other hand shouldn't move all that much.

Inhale normally through your nose, and exhale normally through your mouth. You should breathe deeply enough for your lower abdomen to continue rising and falling. Ten breaths should be taken using this breathing technique in total, or until you start to feel at ease.

If you have trouble breathing from your stomach when standing or sitting up, try lying down and placing a small book on your stomach. As you breathe, try to make the book rise with each inhalation and fall with each exhalation.

Have you heard of it?

Your lungs might remain young if you breathe deeply. If you don't take deep belly breaths at least twice a day, according to Ben Douglas, author of Ageless: Living Younger Longer (Quail Ridge Press, 1990), your lung capacity at age 70 will be barely a third of what it was when you were 20.

Extra Points

Do you consciously breathe in and out each day? Perform the aforementioned workout twice or three times every day to take it to the next level. You could also try the additional deep breathing techniques described below:

1. Maintain a straight back while sitting to ease breathing.
2. Place one hand on your chest, the other on your stomach.
3. Inhale slowly and deeply from your abdomen as you count out loud from one to four.
4. Hold your breath and say out loud the numbers 1 through 7.
5. Completely exhale as you count loudly from 1 to 8. By the time you reach number 8, try to exhale completely.
6. To achieve a relaxed state, repeat three to seven times.

This breathing method, which gets its name from the motion your body makes when you use it, enables you to concentrate on the rhythm of your breathing while expanding your lungs. Start by lying on your back with your knees bent and your feet flat on the floor to complete this exercise.

Your right hand should be on your chest and your left hand should be on your tummy. While maintaining your chest motionless, take a deep breath in through your nose to cause your stomach to rise. Exhale using your mouth. Repeat eight to 10 times.

Continue breathing into your upper chest after your abdomen has fully raised from the inhalation. Do a nose-to-mouth inhalation. Repeat steps 2 eight to ten times. Your chest will rise and your abdomen will progressively fall as you do this.

Your chest and abdomen will initially sag as you slowly exhale through your lips. Feel your body becoming more at ease as you exhale. For three to five minutes, keep breathing in this manner. You can perform this exercise anyplace once you have mastered it on the floor.

Have a Wheatie

Breakfast is the most crucial meal of the day for everyone, whether you're a working parent, a professional on the go, or a student. If you've heard this before and weren't convinced it was true, allow me to reassure you that it is.

According to studies, those who eat breakfast have more energy, perform better in cognitive and memory tasks, and have a lower BMI than people who miss breakfast. A nutritious dinner is also essential for avoiding weariness and preserving steady blood sugar levels.

Although many people skip breakfast in an effort to reduce weight, doing so can be detrimental to your goals. Frequent breakfast consumption is linked to healthier eating habits, better portion control, fewer late-night snacks, and calorie intake that is distributed more evenly throughout the day, all of which support a quick metabolism. However, skipping breakfast has been associated with worse eating patterns, including eating more fat, less fruit, larger meals, and more snacks.

Have you heard of it?

Regular breakfast skippers are 4.5 times more likely to develop obesity. A nutritious breakfast should always be served.

An approach to success

Start the day off right by eating a nutritious breakfast. It promotes better daily routines and boosts top performance. Use the advice below to make sure your breakfast is accomplishing everything it can for your health:

Create Balance: Lean protein, which helps to keep you full throughout the morning, and high-fibre carbohydrates, which give you energy, encourage regularity, and keep you full, should both be included in a nutritious breakfast. Lean meats, such as Canadian bacon or ham, lentils, low- or nonfat milk, yoghurt, and egg whites are all excellent sources of lean protein. Whole grain bread, fruit, oats, and whole grain cereal are among breakfast items that are high in fibre.

Purchase It: Make sure to put breakfast on your weekly shopping list. Include foods that you are confident you will enjoy. A piece of fruit and a low-fat Greek yoghurt are quick options that are simple to make or carry with you if your mornings are frequently busy.

Construct It: Start waking up fifteen to twenty minutes earlier if you have trouble fitting in breakfast time in the mornings. To avoid having to worry about what to cook in the morning, decide what you're going to have for breakfast the night before.

Because they are usually included in breakfast substitutes, it is better to avoid refined sugar and baked goods. Avoid sugary cereals and baked items produced with refined flour, such as bagels, pastries, donuts, muffins, and sugary pastries. These are low in fibre and digest quickly, which causes a spike in blood sugar, a decline in energy, and an increase in hunger an hour or two after eating.

Guidelines for a Healthful Breakfast

Homemade smoothies are tasty, nourishing, and simple to create. To create these, I suggest purchasing a Magic Bullet or compact blender. Here are a few of my favourite foods:

The following chocolate pear recipe calls for smooth, blended ingredients. 1 Anjou apple, which contains 267 calories, 2.8 grams of fat (10% of the total calories), 38.9 grams of carbohydrates, 22.3 grams of protein, and 11.6 grams of fibre; 2 teaspoons of unsweetened cocoa powder, 1/8 cup uncooked oats, 20 g of organic whey protein are present in 2 Tbsp.

one teaspoon of cinnamon water 1/4 cup

Blueberry In your dream, puree the ingredients until they are perfectly smooth. 229 calories are made up of 5 g of fat (20%), 32.3 g of carbohydrates (52%), 15.6 g of protein (28%), and 8 g of fibre. 1 cup of blueberries, wild Greek yoghourt without added sugar, 12 cups, 1/8 cup uncooked oats Ground flaxseed, 1/8 cup, 1 teaspoon and half a cup of cinnamon water. Quick, wholesome breakfasts If making a balanced meal is difficult for you, consider combining any of these simple foods to guarantee that you get both protein and fibre:

Three egg whites, one orange, one piece of whole-grain bread, and one slice of Canadian bacon each contain 225 calories, 3.2 grams of fat, 13% of the calories from carbohydrates, 28.7 grams of carbohydrates, 48% of the calories from protein, 20.5 grams of protein, 39% of the calories from fibre, and 1 cup of skim milk. One half of a banana, one cup of cooked oats, one tablespoon of finely chopped almonds, and one half cup of skim milk each offer 303 calories, 7.5 grams of fat, 21% of carbohydrates, 63%, 13.2 grams of protein, and 6.6 grams of fibre. One apple, one teaspoon of honey, one tablespoon of chopped walnuts, three-quarters cup of nonfat plain Greek yoghurt, and one slice of whole-wheat toast have 301 calories, 6.1 grams of fat, and 4.8 grams of fibre. A homemade concoction The chart below offers recommendations for the three dietary groups—fruit, whole grains, and protein—as well as "extras" that, because of their high fat or sugar content, should be consumed in moderation. In order to make a breakfast that is well-balanced, pick one item from each category:

Extra Points

The breakfast king or queen already? Making breakfast from scratch and using whole-grain flour to produce morning pastries, breads, pancakes, waffles, and muffins can enhance the meal.

Keep It Clean...and Green

Although keeping your house clean is crucial, the method you use matters even more. Today's household cleaners frequently contain toxic substances that could be bad for your family's health as well as your own. Many items contain substances that have been associated with a variety of health problems, including reproductive harm, neurotoxicity, asthma, cancer, and hormone disruption.

Unsafe use of many harsh chemicals can also result in burns to the skin and eyes in addition to lung damage. Use eco-friendly cleaning supplies to get rid of hazardous substances from your home and its surroundings.

An approach to success

Thankfully, cleaners come in more environmentally friendly versions now. But "green washing," or the act of goods firms making claims about their products that aren't entirely accurate, is a common practice. Consequently, making wise decisions while buying greener products pays off: Damaging criminals You can become a more savvy consumer and will know what to look for in the products you are considering buying if you are aware of which ingredients are the most harmful to you and your family. See, kindly While there are numerous dangerous compounds that should be avoided, cleaning agents are the worst offenders.

Perform analysis Many labels on cleaning supplies and pesticides do not give you the complete picture since manufacturers are not required to list all of the components in their products. Calling the business and requesting an extensive ingredient list is the best line of action. You may also search for the product on the manufacturer's website. For fresh, current information on a range of laws, regulations, goods, and substances, you can also check out the websites of the Environmental Working Group (www.ewg.org) and the Environmental Protection Agency (www.epa.gov).

Constituents with varying levels of toxicity Variously hazardous chemicals can be found in many items. For example, the phrases "surfactants" and "preservatives" are not entirely clear and do not describe the categories of compounds they relate to. Try to avoid buying anything that contains them as a result.

Gain Certification When in uncertainty Every day, new products are released onto the market. Furthermore, a lot of people exaggerate the safety of their products to sell them even though they aren't. Choose environmentally friendly products, such as those that are Green Seal or EcoLogo certified (www.environmental choice.com).

Past events must end: Look at all the cleaning supplies and insecticides you currently own by going through your cabinets. Bring items containing the compounds to a nearby hazardous waste site for disposal if they are specified in Cleaning Components to Avoid. The hazardous compounds listed should not be flushed down the toilet since they are bad for the environment and wildlife.

Extra Points

Utilise any green items in your home already? Using homemade cleansers will result in more thorough cleaning. These options are said to be the safest and greenest ones. For some of the most popular household goods with cleaning qualities, refer to the substances listed in Safe Household Cleaning chemicals.

Use the following DIY recipes for different cleaning solutions even though they are not an exhaustive list. Please be aware that while implementing these recipes can help you use fewer hazardous materials in your house, specific outcomes may differ. Test your answers in secluded, limited settings and exercise caution at all times. Children should not have access to any marked formulations that are kept in storage.

In the kitchen, combine one part vinegar to one part water for surfaces (other than stone or marble). Use the solution to scrub the surfaces.

Surfaces like countertops and others Sprinkle baking soda on the counters and wipe them down with a wet sponge to clean them. Additionally effective on stainless steel refrigerators, chopping boards, oven tops, and sinks.

Microwave two tablespoons of baking soda in a mug of water until it starts to boil. Apply the solution to interior surfaces and rub. Washing machine detergent. Half a cup of vinegar should be added to the dishwasher's detergent container. proceed as usual.

Dishes. Lemons should be cut in half, with baking soda placed on the cut side. Lemon is used to wash the dishes.

Waste Removal Deodorizer. Use the garbage disposal to get rid of any leftover lemon (or orange) peel. Turn on until the act of grinding uses no water. Rinse after 10 minutes of letting it sit.

Baking soda can be kept in the refrigerator with the lid open as a deodorizer.

to maintain ovens A paste formed of baking soda and water should be placed in the oven. Overnight, leave the paste on the surface. scrub the following day. Use a wet sponge or towel to clean.

On bathroom surfaces that have mildew, use vinegar or lemon juice. After letting it stand for a little while, scrub with a hard brush. Every week, add three cups of vinegar to the rear tank and three cups to the toilet to keep the bowl clean.

Drains: Pour a cup of baking soda and a cup of vinegar down a clogged drain to clear it. Wait 15 minutes before running hot water down the drain. For obstinate clogs, repeat.

Mirrors and windows are examples of surfaces. One litre of water and two teaspoons of white vinegar should be put in a spray bottle. Mirrors and windows can be cleaned with a spray and a cloth. On the paper towels, there is a streak.

Streak-free Windows and Mirrors: Fill a spray bottle with a quart of water and 1/4 cup cornstarch. Mirrors and windows should be sprayed, then wiped with a dry terry towel until sparkling and dry.

Wooden flooring. Spray bottle needs to be filled with 1/4 cup of white vinegar and 30 ounces of warm water. Use a wet mop and the solution to wipe the floors.

Your Cereal Should Contain The Entire Grain

All grains start out whole. Because they contain all the elements of the seed and are rich in fibre, protein, and minerals, whole grains are satisfying and nutrient-dense. Additionally, studies have shown that whole grain diets—as opposed to ones heavy in refined grains—help lower the risk of developing a number of chronic illnesses, including colon cancer, stroke, type 2 diabetes, heart disease, asthma, inflammatory diseases, and tooth loss. Finally, whole grains help maintain a healthy weight, decrease cholesterol, and control blood sugar and blood pressure levels.

Many items, including a range of breads, pastas, cereals, and baked products, are made with refined grains and flours. The bran and germ are taken from grains during refinement, reducing the amount of fibre, protein, and other nutrients in the grain. Refined grains are transformed into low-nutrient, empty-calorie foods that make you nauseous and unpleasant.

The Change: Choose whole grains over processed ones.

The news, you say? Even if you have celiac disease or gluten intolerance, you can still consume whole grains. The grains that don't contain gluten include amaranth, buckwheat, corn, millet, quinoa, rice, sorghum, teff, and wild rice.

A strategy for success

The recommended daily intake of whole grains is three servings (48 grams). One serving contains the following whole grains:

1. 12 cups of brown rice, barley, or some other grain, cooked
2. 12 cups of whole-grain pasta that has been fully cooked
3. Hot, ready-made oats in 12 cups porridge
4. A single serving of whole grain-only cold cereal or a single piece of whole grain bread

A List of Grains Whole grains exist in a variety of varieties besides wheat, rice, and oats. Other varieties include: Besides Quinoa, Brown Rice, Rye, Sorghum,

Spelt, Teff, and Triticale Wheat, other grains include Barley, Amaranth, Buckwheat, Bulgur, Corn, Farro, Emmer Grano, Kamut, Millet, and Oats.

Identifying text: False marketing claims are made on the packaging of several foods. Common terms like "multigrain" and "wheat flour" don't always make it apparent when whole grains are used in a recipe. You may ensure that your diet is rich in whole grains by following the suggestions below:

Stamps with granules: The Whole Grains Council produced two stamps in 2005 to help customers identify products that contain whole grains. The "Basic Whole Grain Stamp" is placed on products that contain at least eight grams of whole grains per serving. Keep in mind that products with this certification may contain certain upgraded components. A product with the "100% Whole Grain Stamp" means that it is produced entirely of whole grains, includes at least one serving, and each serving has at least 16 grams of whole grains.

If the product does not have a stamp from the Whole Grains Council, check the ingredient list. To find out which ingredients are whole, which ones are questionable, and which ones aren't even formed of whole grains, have a look at the chart under "How Whole Grain Is It?" on the following page.

Start eating breakfast cereal made with nourishing grains. Look for the Whole Grains Council Stamp and a list of the ingredients that are made of whole grains on labels. High-fibre breakfast options include plain steel-cut or rolled oats, unsweetened shredded wheat, unsweetened bran flakes, muesli, and any other cereal. For a healthy yogurtparfait, combine some raw oats, fruit, and plain, nonfat Greek yoghurt.

Bagels: For toast and sandwiches, whole-wheat or whole-grain bread is preferable than white bread. Additional choices include whole-wheat bagels and English muffins. Choose whole-wheat pita bread instead of white pita bread and whole-wheat tortillas in place of white flour tortillas for healthier wraps.

Using Grains in Recipes: The flavours of unprocessed and processed grains differ. However, as you get used to the flavour difference, you'll probably realise that you prefer foods made from whole grains to those made from flour and refined grains. If you discover that making the complete transition is difficult, start by substituting half of the refined grains with whole grains to give your taste receptors some time to adjust. reduce the amount of the refined option while gradually switching to the whole grain alternative:

White rice should be swapped out for brown, kasha, or whole-wheat bulgur. Brown rice can be prepared on its own or in salads, casseroles, soups, and stews along with other ingredients.

Replace ordinary pasta with whole-wheat or whole-grain types. Use only whole-grain or whole-wheat flour varieties for cooking. Use whole-wheat pastry flour that has been finely milled to give your dishes or baked items a lighter texture.

Use whole-grain bread wherever breadcrumbs are called for in a recipe. You may make your own whole-grain bread crumbs if you can't locate any by slicing whole-grain bread into crumbs and toasting the crumbs in the oven.

as well Meat: Three-quarters of a cup of uncooked oats, whole-grain breadcrumbs, or cooked brown rice can all improve meatballs, burgers, or meatloaf. Try making whole-grain salads with quinoa, barley, or tabbouleh (made with bulgur made from broken wheat).

For the Whole Grains Council, extra credit

You must already include whole grains in your meals, I'll suppose. Take it a step further by using the advice in the following paragraphs:

Date of Meal Unless a restaurant's menu clearly states that the dishes are made with 100 percent whole wheat or whole grains, you can presume that breads, pastas, desserts, and pastries are made with refined grains. However, eating establishments are starting to give in to customer desires for healthier food. Nowadays, there are additional options available, like whole-wheat pizza crusts, brown rice served with sushi, and whole-wheat pastas. Before placing your order, make sure whole grain options are available.

Look into New Grains: Try some of the grains that were listed at the beginning of this week's Roadmap for Success. Look up recipes online for ideas on delectable new dishes.

Attempting baking Moving from refined to whole-grain flours can be a little more difficult in baking than it is in cooking. Start by substituting whole-wheat flour for white flour for baking cookies, muffins, quick breads, and pancakes. Along with other flours, try using whole cornmeal, spelt, bran, and oat flours. When baking with whole-grain flours, the consistency may alter. As a result, start by substituting only half the amount unless you have experience baking with whole-grain flours.

A loud laugh

Newborns and infants don't start smiling and laughing until a few months after birth. However, many of us begin to lose some of our natural chuckles and laughter as we get older. Growing responsibilities, routines, interactions with problematic relatives, or everyday difficulties could all contribute to some of it. Unfortunately, this lack of laughter may have an adverse effect on our health.

Laughter is good for our bodies, minds, and interpersonal relationships. It strengthens our heart, relieves pain, and strengthens our immune system on a physical level. Our bodies release endorphins, commonly referred to as "happy hormones," when we laugh, while stress hormones like cortisol, adrenaline, and dopamine are repressed. When we laugh, we strengthen our diaphragm, stomach, and core muscles as well as blood flow and blood vessel function.

Laughter improves our perspective and disposition, lessens fear and anxiety, and makes overcoming challenges and trying circumstances easier. It enhances our quality of life, provides us more energy, and strengthens our resistance to stress. We can turn our focus from negative emotions like anger, resentment, and worry to pleasant ones by laughing. It provides a cleansing emotional release that allows us to shift from a very serious to a comic point of view.

The fact that laughter is a spontaneous activity in and of itself allows us to let go of inhibitions, be in the moment, and express our true emotions. Because it allows us to pull back, be more creative, and come up with answers more quickly and effectively, humour also helps us solve problems.

Not to mention the beneficial social advantages of laughter. Laughter strengthens our bonds with one another, reduces tension, and promotes stronger interpersonal relationships. A typical "feel good" stress release produces positive emotions, strengthens emotional ties, and improves social interactions.

If you haven't been enjoying the 25 Small Changes thus far, be ready to enjoy this week's change and have fun. Every day, make it a point to smile.

A strategy for success

Of all the changes you make this year, this one should be the easiest and most joyful. Who could dispute the delight of laughter, after all? If you haven't already, attempt to incorporate laughing into each day of your life.

Let's start by grinning: A smile triggers the beginning of a chuckle. A chuckle can only start with a smile. Aim to grin more frequently. Smile to people you see on the street as you pass. Smile when you see something lovely. Smile when you are with loved ones or pals. Increase the number of smiles you display on a daily basis.

Playfulness should permeate your surroundings. Spend time with those that have a natural sense of comedy and energy. You'll get happier and lighter as a result of noticing it. Both kids and dogs can make us smile, laugh, and offer us a reason to unwind and enjoy ourselves. With those that are very serious or who have a negative outlook, you'll probably laugh less.

Become Less Serious About Yourself: When you behave poorly or make mistakes, try not to be too hard on yourself. Instead, share your embarrassing tales with others and laugh them off. This will improve your relationship with yourself as well as your attitude toward and appeal to other people. You probably know someone who is incredibly serious about life and oneself. They probably aren't fun to be around. To help you avoid acting like that person, you should occasionally remind yourself of them.

Forget the seriousness: Although some life situations, like death, necessitate seriousness, most of them don't. Find humour in tough or uncomfortable situations. By seeking for them, you can learn to enjoy life's ironies rather than finding them upsetting. Many aspects of life are beyond our control, most notably other people's behaviour. The things (and people) that irritate, anger, or even insult you can be laughed at. You can improve your attitude on life and lessen stress by doing this. Think about the following to alter your viewpoint: Is it even worthwhile to voice outrage over this? Do I care about it at all? Is it truly as bad as I'm making it out to be? Is it really that important?

Reduced Stress Laughter and stress do not mix well. To offer yourself more room for humour, learn to manage your stress in a healthy way. Add entertaining activities: Increase the amount of time you spend playing, and take part in pleasurable, lighthearted activities. For example, watch more movies than tragedies. observe a comic club. Read the comics in the newspaper. Play video games with your friends. Look into comedic books. By telling jokes and encouraging others to do the same, you may spread comedy. Ask your pals what funny things have happened to them recently. Play mini golf, go on the rides, bowl, and sing along. Pose in a playful manner!

Lie Whenever there is doubt If smiling and laughing come naturally to you, work on them a little. Nobody wants to appear to be lying. Pretend to smile and laugh in the privacy of your own house. It might get easier to chuckle when a true circumstance arises as you laugh more frequently.

The news, you say? Your muscles may continue to relax and your tension level may decrease for up to 45 minutes after you stop laughing.

Extra Credit

Have you already mastered the art of laughing? To take it farther, make them chuckle. You and your loved ones will become closer if you laugh more. If you have a particularly good sense of humour, you might even want to consider stand-up comedy or taking a comedy class.

Get Five Squares Per Day

We usually have to stop what we are doing in order to focus on eating, which is one of the nicest things about life.

My Own Story: Eating excessively, insufficiently, or skipping meals can slow down your metabolism, make you feel continually peckish, or make you feel uncomfortably "overstuffed." However, keeping a regular eating pattern is very beneficial to your health.

Among other things, optimising your eating habits will offer you more control over your hunger. Your body won't experience bouts of extreme hunger if you spread out your meals throughout the day. Additionally, regular eating makes sure you're giving your body the nutrients and energy it needs to function, which enables you to be active and productive.

Not to mention that eating speeds up metabolism because digesting, absorbing, and metabolising food all demand energy. On the other hand, if you spend too long without eating, your metabolism may slow down since your body will think you are starving. Establish a daily eating schedule that you will enjoy.

A strategy for success

We all have different ways of boosting the health advantages of our meals. However, the majority of specialists agree that most men and women benefit from eating a few snacks in between bigger main meals. It could take some getting accustomed to eating five or six times a day, but as you get used to it, you'll notice that your energy levels are more consistent throughout the day and that you have greater control over your appetite. Here are some tips:

Everything begins with breakfast: It is crucial to start your day with a healthy, well-balanced meal, as we previously covered in Week 13—Eat Your Wheaties. According to studies, people who regularly have a filling breakfast weigh less than those who don't. After an hour and a half of awakening, be sure to consume a wholesome meal.

Boost Snacks While Cutting Back on Main Meals: At each meal, you should consume fewer calories overall and reserve some for snacks. An example of a good eating schedule to follow:

1. Breakfast is served between 6:30 and 8:00 am.
2. Snack in the late morning: 9:30–10:30 a.m. Lunch until 1:30 p.m.
3. 4:00–5:00 p.m. is prime snack time.
4. From 6:00 to 7:30 p.m. is dinnertime.

In advance: Keep in mind that skipping meals will make your metabolism slow down and increase your desire for food. When this occurs, you could overeat and are more prone to make poor decisions. Bring tasty, satisfying, and healthy snacks with you if you anticipate being on the road all day or if your schedule is busy. Whole fruit, unsalted almonds, and energy bars like Kind Bars or Lara Bars are simple snacks to pack. If your schedule is erratic, be sure to always have some snacks on hand so you can relax when necessary.

What about some food? A busy day is one thing, but if you anticipate having a busy week, prepare lots of food on Sunday so you have ready-to-eat meals all week. If you want to avoid becoming too accustomed to your alternatives, you could attempt to cook a few different healthy recipes.

Makes You Shiver

Inactivity destroys everyone's health, whereas movement and intentional exercise preserve it. It's likely that you expected this change to be one of the 25 Small Changes. Regular cardiovascular exercise is one of the best ways to keep young for years to come. It increases your energy and stamina during the day and encourages deeper sleep at night. Through the release of endorphins and other mood-enhancing substances, aerobic exercise improves your disposition and attitude.

Additionally, it aids in lowering anxiety and depression. People who engage in aerobic exercise can control their weight and lower their body fat. Regular cardiovascular exercise strengthens the heart and lungs the most as a result of the increased heart rate and oxygen intake. The prevention of illnesses including high blood pressure, diabetes, obesity, and heart disease depends on maintaining a regular aerobic exercise regimen. To perform a regular aerobic activity, raise your heart rate to between 60 and 80% of your maximal heart rate for 30 minutes, three times each week.

I've heard the news. Because it can improve one's overall fitness, energy, self-esteem, and body image, regular exercise is linked to better sex.

A strategy for success

The best way to begin an aerobic fitness program is to keep things simple. For you to continue exercising, it must be pleasurable, advantageous, and convenient; otherwise, you won't. When you react too rapidly or become involved too soon, you run a greater risk of self-harm or agitation. Finally, if you haven't been exercising frequently, talk to your doctor before starting a new fitness routine.

Consider a Fun Action: Contrary to what many people think, there are numerous effective aerobic workout techniques. Running for miles on end is not required. It's crucial to keep your heart rate rising steadily for 30 minutes. As long as you follow through with this, you are free to do everything you want, including chasing your kids around the yard. Common aerobic exercises include walking, jogging, bicycling, dancing, hiking, rollerblading, boxing, swimming, tennis, and aerobics classes. Make a list of your best options to begin with, then work your way up from there.

It would be simple to live by the adage that if something is difficult or time-consuming, even if you truly want to do it, you probably won't. Mark the items on your list that are the most useful as you go over it once more. You must focus on these during the initial weeks of this adjustment.

If you're just starting out, walking is a physical activity that can be done almost anyplace. For the wonderful activity known as power walking, all you need are your workout clothing and sneakers. There is nothing new you need to learn because you already know how to walk.

Keep the following in mind: Make plans and set aside time each week for exercise. Planning encourages behavioural change by ensuring that you allot enough time and holding you responsible for achieving your goals. Choose three days this week to work out aerobically. In your calendar or planner, make a note of the specifics, such as the day, hour, place, time, and activity you intend to carry out. So that you have no room for error or to change your course of action, make sure you are properly attired and wearing the suitable footwear. When deciding when to work out, use common sense. If you know you won't be as likely to complete your workout as you will at night, don't schedule it for the morning.

Understanding Intensity Levels When starting an exercise program, exercise on its own is beneficial. You must build up to a high enough intensity before you can experience the results. To determine how hard you're working out, try one of the activities below.

Analysing the conversation: You must demonstrate during the talk exam that you can carry on a conversation while exercising. If you are having difficulty speaking, reduce the pressure. However, you're probably not working hard enough if you can talk to someone without your breathing shifting. Engage in enough rigorous exercise to make communication difficult but not impossible.

Sincere Effort With this method, you keep an eye on how your body feels as you workout to determine how much effort you are putting forth. If you feel like you are pushing yourself, your heart rate is up, and you are sweating, you are surely getting good exercise. However, you're probably not working out hard enough if you don't feel like you're making much effort, your heart rate feels only slightly or not at all higher, or you hardly perspire.

Monitoring your heart rate is the most accurate and effective way to determine how hard you're working during exercise. You can take your pulse if you don't have a heart rate monitor. To determine how intense your workout was, take your pulse after exerting yourself for around 10 minutes. Right now, for ten seconds, take your pulse in one of the following locations:

Most frequently, people feel their neck for their pulse. Put your middle and index fingers under your ear and under your jawline. Exactly behind the side of your chin, in the hollow of your neck, place your fingers. You should be able to feel your pulse at this stage.

The Hand Make sure your left hand's palm is pointing up. Place the middle and index fingers of your right hand at the centre of the upward-facing part of your left wrist. You should be able to feel your pulse at this stage.

After determining your pulse, count your heartbeats for 10 seconds. Check your pulse to see if it is between the 60% and 80% values for the age on the chart below that most closely matches your own. Furthermore, one-minute counts are provided:

If your pulse is below the 60% column percentage during your workout, you should exert more effort. Exercise less intensely if your pulse rate is higher than the proportion in the 80% column.

Record Your Activities in a Journal: Even if it wasn't scheduled on your calendar, keep a note of every workout you complete. Utilise Fitday.com to monitor your dietary intake and activity schedule. If you approach it in this way, you'll be able to keep track of all you've accomplished with nutrition and exercise. Make a note of the activities you undertook, along with their duration and level of difficulty. If you would rather journal by hand, use the Activity Log, which is provided in Part III—Tools and Resources.

Maintaining Motivation You'll surely start to like working out more if you make it a daily ritual. You'll start to feel less stressed and more physically able to perform your daily tasks. Additionally, you'll begin to feel better about your appearance. But initially, you might need a little more nagging. The following suggestions might be helpful:

Turn on some music. Buy an MP3 player or iPod Shuffle. With an emphasis on upbeat and danceable music, compile a playlist of your favourite songs to listen to while working out. If you listen to peppy music, you might be inspired to carry on even when you don't feel like it. If you listen to sluggish or quiet music, you could lose your excitement and vitality.

Develop connections You might find it easier to keep motivated and to support someone else's weight loss goals if you exercise with a friend or family member. Make sure your workout companion is someone you can rely on to inspire and motivate you when you need it most. They must also be trustworthy and dependable.

Purchase the Best Tools: For exercising, always dress appropriately. Anything that is extremely saggy, loose, constricting, or tight is not what you desire. Women should get at least two pairs of supportive sports bras to wear underneath their training clothes. If you plan to exercise outside, be sure your workout attire is suited for the weather. Buy a nice pair of shoes to make sure your feet are protected and cushioned.

Putting the Advantages First On days when you are particularly unmotivated, keep in mind the benefits of exercise. Think about the benefits of success. Remind yourself of the advantages of both short-term enhanced mood and stress alleviation as well as long-term improved health and disease prevention.

Already engage in three 30-minute sessions per week of exercise Extra Points? Use these suggestions to facilitate it:

Improve It: You can up your activity level by working out more frequently or for longer periods of time. Think about extending your workout from thirty to forty minutes. Alternately, increase your weekly workout schedule from three to four or five.

When engaging in aerobic exercise, challenge yourself to perform things you've never done before. Join a team sport, sign up for a new exercise class at a club, or go biking with friends or coworkers. To keep you interested, make sure everything is fresh and fascinating.

Diversify: Research has shown that varying your exercise routines will improve your performance and reduce your risk of injury, even though repetitive exercise is still superior to idleness. If you normally walk, think about varying your exercise routine by periodically climbing and descending stadium steps on an elliptical trainer, a bike, or a Stairmaster.

Motivate yourself. To challenge yourself, set a new goal for yourself. Take part in a half-marathon or a triathlon. Participate in a race to raise money for a good cause. Create a running club. Find new ways to challenge yourself to keep yourself interesting and motivated.

Request for Fruit Eaters

Fruits and vegetables both promote and preserve great health. They are also loaded with phytonutrients, fibre, vitamins, and minerals that help fight disease, obesity, and ageing, as was described in Week 8—Eat Your Vegetables. Antioxidants, sometimes referred to as phytonutrients, are particularly beneficial in disarming poisons that harm cells and may result in health issues.

Fruits' hues reflect the phytonutrients they contain in a manner similar to how vegetables' colours do. The Every Color of the Rainbow chart has been updated to reflect the fruit's colour classification on the following page. Due to the natural colours inherent in fruit as opposed to vegetables, some phytonutrients are easier to find in fruit than in vegetables, and vice versa.

Because fruit generally has vibrant red, blue, and purple hues, anthocyanins and lycopene are more frequently found in fruit than in vegetables. However, because there are so many veggies that naturally have a green tint, you'll discover that the nutrients found in green plant foods are easier to find in vegetables than in fruit. This is why a balanced diet should include both fruits and vegetables. It is advised to consume two to four portions of fruit per day rather than four to six portions of fibrous vegetables because fruit has more calories per serving than these vegetables.

Each day, consume two to four servings of whole fruit. One serving is equivalent to one cup of fruit (such as berries) or one medium fruit (such as a grapefruit or half of a banana).

An approach to success

It shouldn't be too challenging to include fruit in your day because the entire fruit is portable and simple to take with you. Here are some suggestions to make it simple for you to consume the two to four servings per day that are advised:

First, pick your favourite: For an illustration, have a look at the food described in Every Color of the Rainbow—Fruit. Make a decision and start adding your preferred fruit into your daily activities.

Experiment: Try new fruit varieties every week, just like with fibrous veggies. Once more, look online for healthy recipe websites before preparing or including fruit in recipes.

Get ready for the coming week by: Fruit should be on your grocery list, and you should buy enough to last the entire week.

Purchase before ripe. It's best to choose fruit that isn't quite ripe if you're buying it for the week. By doing this, you can prevent the fruit from becoming bad or turning mushy before you eat it. A banana will seem somewhat green and still have a firm texture if it is underripe.

Fruit is a naturally occurring component of a healthy breakfast. Add a cup of blueberries or a half-banana on top of your cereal or oatmeal. Instead of drinking orange juice, eat an orange. Alternatively, you could whip up a wonderful smoothie with fruit and protein for a quick breakfast you could take with you.

The Relationship between Fruit, Sugar, and Cravings

Our bodies' natural tendency is to seek sugar, as do our minds. Our ancestors were biologically drawn to the sweetness of fruit because it contained micronutrients that avoided sickness, improved immunity, and were essential to health even before humans learned to refine sugar. Because eating sweet foods causes the release of serotonin, a neurotransmitter that influences our sense of wellbeing and controls our mood, sleep patterns, and hunger, we have an emotional craving for sugar.

Because of this, our body loves sugar and needs the vitamins, energy, and endorphins that come from eating fruit. So, the next time you crave something sweet, try eating some fruit. It could be exactly what your body and mind need.

Salads during lunch and dinner can be made sweeter by adding fruit. Oranges, grapefruit, apples, pears, raspberries, strawberries, blueberries, grapes, and raisins are some fruits that go nicely in salads.

Sandwiches: Sandwiches taste sweet and salty when they are made with slices of apple or pears and a little cheese. Instead of potato chips, potato salad, French fries, or macaroni salad, choose sliced oranges, apples, or a fresh fruit salad to go with your sandwich.

Dessert: As a post-meal treat, opt for a piece of fruit and a little amount of extra-dark chocolate (70 percent cacao content or more) rather than grabbing a cookie or slice of pie.

What's in the bowl for snacks? We frequently select the goods that will be most beneficial as snacks. Fruit ought to come first over bad foods like chips and desserts. Apples, bananas, oranges, grapes, pears, cherries, and tangerines are a few examples of fruit that doesn't require refrigeration. Place these fruits in a dish on the table. Additionally, stock up on fruit for your everyday mid-morning or early-afternoon office snacks.

Easily Combinable Consider mixing some of these components for a filling, vitamin- and mineral-rich snack if you're short on time:

1. 1/4 cup of almonds and a pear
2. A slice of whole-grain bread with an apple slice on top.
3. One-half of a banana and one tablespoon of peanut butter
4. Supplements and concentrates of antioxidant juice

Antioxidant dietary supplements are now much more widely available. In addition to the aforementioned vitamins and minerals, fresh fruits and vegetables also provide other naturally occurring benefits that are lost when those nutrients are removed and processed into bottled, pill, or powder form. Remain true to the source and make an effort to consume as many fruits and vegetables in their entire form as you can.

Have you heard of it?

Fruit juices, especially those made entirely of juice, tend to be high in calories and low in fibre when compared to whole fruit. Juice consumption may consequently result in an increase in blood sugar levels. For instance, compared to a glass of orange juice's 85 calories and lack of fibre, a single orange has roughly 65 calories and 3 grams of fibre. Since whole fruit is more filling and takes longer to digest than juice, it is better at controlling blood sugar and energy levels.

Extra Points

Already a fruit addict? Increase the tempo: Variety of Stress: Eating a variety of fruit hues is beneficial, much like eating a lot of vegetables. Try to eat at least two servings of each colour of the rainbow each week.

Encourage your friends, family, and children: Encourage your family, friends, or roommates to eat fruit as a nutritious snack. While watching TV, share a bowl of cherries with someone. Give a coworker some grapes. Make berry sundaes with the help of your kids for dessert.

Live With A Purpose

Since life is such a beautiful gift, being alive is a blessing. Take a moment to consider how incredible it is that you are here in this vast universe and across all of time, despite the fact that it may sound cliche. Observe life, breathe, and learn. A purpose provides our existence meaning and a reason to exist, and that much is certain. We are unable to fully understand many facets of existence.

When we live with a purpose, we actively work to build the kind of life we want—one that is significant and meaningful. It encourages us to accept accountability for the deeds, choices, and directions we make in life and makes it possible for us to be mind-independent. Our character and the legacy we leave behind are what matter most, not our material goods or our jobs. Living with passion and purpose enables us to find our mission in life and build the life we want. It also clarifies our identity and reinforces our fundamental convictions. It also helps us to better understand what is most essential to us.

Additionally, having a goal keeps us from feeling "stuck" in life. It urges us to seize the day and live regretfully, or even worse, to lead lives that are motivated by fear. It influences the way we think, feel, and act. When things get tough, purpose gives us the strength to keep going and move forward while still being the best versions of ourselves. Discover your life's mission and live it every day.

An approach to success

Your life's work is unique, just like the way you found it and carried it out. It unquestionably takes a completely different action than your friends, family, or workplace. It can take some time to discover and pursue your life's purpose, and it may change throughout the course of your existence:

Self-discovery

Self-discovery is the first step to achieving your objective. It's crucial to comprehend oneself, one's ideals, and one's priorities. To achieve this, start by responding to the questions below:

What Are You Seeking? Take some time, no matter your age, to think about what you want in life. As you do this, try not to think about anything or anyone else. Only you are aware of the solution. You shouldn't base your response to this question on your fears, grudges, or wrath. Additionally, refrain from responding to this crucial topic out of a need for affirmation or a desire to impress others. Instead, consider your goals for your life and who you want to become. To learn more, think about the following questions:

1. What will I want to have accomplished in my lifetime when I'm 70, 80, or 90?
2. What would I want a child to think of me if I had one?
3. What would I want my grandchildren to think of me if I had any?
4. What would I want to say in my eulogy if I were to pass away?
5. What would I want people to say about me if I were to die?
6. What is necessary for me to be
7. Happy and content in life
8. Joyous
9. Fulfilled?
10. What Motivates You?

It's time to think about your interests now that you are aware of what you want from life. Your source of inspiration and sense of direction comes from your activities. These are the things that make you happy and joyful. They are the acts you carry out willingly and without remorse. You have no choice but to carry them out, regardless of reward or acclaim.

How Do You Become a Strong Person? Now is the moment to appreciate your benefits. What skills do you have? What talent do you have that others don't? Our areas of interest and strength typically, although not always, coincide. You can, for example, have a great love for music but be tone deaf. As a result, your musical talent might not be as powerful.

On the other hand, if you have a keen interest in the environment and are good at writing and diplomacy, you might be the ideal candidate for environmental policy. This query should receive entirely automated responses. You are aware of your accomplishments and weaknesses. Re-examine the list of your advantages you made in Part III—Tools and Resources.

What Is Most Important to You? What cause, if any, would you pledge your devotion to? What makes you queasy in the stomach? Do you want to make changes to your neighbourhood or the planet we live in? Are there any specific factors that motivate you to take action?

Personal Purpose Statement: Create one

Business mission statements give a detailed explanation of the goals and objectives of the organisation. This provides the business a purpose and ensures that every action they take sends the same message. In essence, their brand is defined by their mission statement. Try to create your mission statement now that you are more aware of who you are. Explain your idea of your life's purpose in a few phrases or fewer.

Include everything you just thought of, such as your objectives, passions, expertise, and most important causes. How did you get here? What do you want to impart to the world? What type of impact are you hoping to have? What motivates you to get out of bed? This declaration ought to be something you can relate to, feel proud of, and serve as a sensible and useful guide for your decisions and deeds in life.

Include this phrase in the Tools and Resources section of the Purpose and Mission Statement in Part III. Franklin Covey's Mission Statement Builder is an excellent tool for crafting your personal mission statement if you need a bit more direction.

Plan Ahead

The next stage is to create a plan with the intention of attaining your purpose and goals. Set goals for yourself after giving thought to the meaning of your life. Big dreams, bravery, and most importantly, self-confidence! How would you like to be recalled? Consider the actions you must take to accomplish your objectives. Your life will be easier to manage and you'll be able to continue on a meaningful route even if your goals alter over time. You will be better able to judge which course of action is best for you when opportunities arise because you will be able to determine if they are compatible with your strategy.

Have you heard of it?

People who can sum up their life's purpose in one sentence are 20% happier than those who can't, according to Dan Buettner of the Blue Zones.

Living Your Objectives and Goals

Be Firm and Decisive: You're making a deliberate decision to live a purposeful life. Your personal purpose statement and strategy should be periodically reviewed because they are dynamic. Keep in mind that finding your purpose in life has less to do with your job or the "have-tos" of life and more to do with your choices, social contributions, and personal identity.

Accept change: You, the world, and your circumstances will all change as time goes on. This entire process is a common occurrence in life. However, everything hinges on your response. Understand that being flexible will enable you to adjust as necessary as circumstances change. Maintain your dedication to your primary objectives while making any required adjustments to your plan.

Daily Exercise: The more consciously you live, the more it will come naturally to you. Remind yourself of your commitment each day. Read your mission statement as soon as you get out of bed. Find out what your daily objectives are and how you plan to achieve them.

Extra Points

I assume you already heed your calling. Give the money out! encourage people to lead meaningful lives. Create a family mission statement or collaborate with others to create a team mission statement. Work with people to make living a meaningful, purpose-driven life a reality by educating them on its importance.

Keep It Pure

Whether or not you shop at Whole Foods, it's likely that you are becoming more and more knowledgeable about the organic movement. Organic has expanded significantly beyond food. Even some could contend that it has gone too far. Consumer products, personal care items, home goods, and even apparel are making organic claims increasingly frequently. Whatever your opinion of the organic movement as a whole, it is difficult to dispute the advantages of organic in terms of our food supply and agricultural methods.

The differences between conventional and organic farming are numerous. First, organic farming employs natural nutrients like manure or compost, whereas conventional farming uses chemical fertilisers to grow plants. Organic farming uses beneficial insects and birds, mating disruption, or traps to eliminate pests and disease while conventional farming uses chemicals to control pests.

Additionally, conventional farming uses chemical herbicides to control weeds, whereas organic farming relies on mulch, tilling, hand weeding, and adequate crop rotation. In traditional livestock husbandry, animals are administered antibiotics, growth hormones, and medications to prevent sickness and promote their development. They are also confined, which limits or completely eliminates their capacity to move or graze. None of these practices are permitted in organic animal husbandry, which also uses methods to prevent disease and gives animals access to the outdoors so they can roam more freely as they were intended to.

How Much Money Do Organic Products Really Save You?

Many people wonder whether spending extra money on organic food is worthwhile. In a nutshell, yes. The case for purchasing organic products is strong. According to the USDA, organic food is produced without synthetic fertilisers, antibiotics, growth hormones, pesticides, or feed derived from animal organs, all of which have the potential to be harmful to human health. This is especially true for kids, who are more susceptible to these harmful chemicals, as well as for pregnant or nursing women, who might pass these toxins on to developing foetuses or newborns.

From a production standpoint, organic farming assures that grains, fruits, and vegetables are cultivated without the use of pesticides. Many of the pesticides still in use today were approved by the Environmental Protection Agency years before they were connected to cancer, blood, liver, kidney, and other illnesses. The EPA estimates that 30% of insecticides, 60% of fungicides, and 90% of herbicides have cancer-causing potential. The USDA has discovered that conventionally farmed fruit still contains a significant amount more pesticide residue than produce grown organically, even after washing. Research has shown that organic produce has a higher nutritional content and better flavour than produce cultivated conventionally, which is another reason to pick it.

When referring to animal products, the phrase "organic" denotes that no antibiotics, growth hormones, or rbGH were administered to the animals during their whole growing process, nor were any animal parts included in their diet. This is significant, especially for beef producers, as cows that consume animal feed containing animal carcasses may get mad cow disease, which can be lethal to humans. And while growth hormones have been related to an increased risk of cancer, the use of antibiotics in animals has been connected to the emergence of bacteria resistant to them. Finally, many organic farms handle their animals more humanely from the standpoint of animal welfare. For goods made from animals that had access to the great outdoors and weren't kept in cages, look for labels like "free-range" and "ranch raised."

The environment also benefits from organic farming. Organic agricultural methods aid in preserving the harmony needed for a healthy ecology. Instead of degrading soils and harming water supplies, organic agriculture practices aim to improve topsoil and safeguard groundwater. Animals play a crucial role in the organic farming process of naturally fertilising the soil, yet on industrial farms, enormous amounts of manure contaminate wells with infections like E. coli. Not to mention that industrial farms consume a lot of energy, which is harmful to the environment, and rely on inexpensive, nonrenewable fossil fuels. Purchase organic meat, produce, and other products wherever possible.

An approach to success

Organic food may initially cost more, but since it is better for your health, you will likely end up saving money if you do. If you adhere to the following advice, you can choose organic products wisely:

Verify the Label: To be advertised as organic, food goods must adhere to USDA regulations. USDA certification is required before a farmer or food producer can label a product as organic. Produce, eggs, or other goods with only one component must all be 100 percent organic in order for the USDA to certify them as organic. A food item must be at least 95% organic if it is processed or prepared.

The Clean 15 and The Dirty Dozen The majority of lettuces, thin-skinned fruits and vegetables like apples, pears, and berries, as well as vegetables and fruits with thin skins like spinach, peppers, and potatoes, tend to retain pesticides even after washing. On the other side, vegetables like onions and corn with "layered" or heartier skins tend to be safer, as do fruits with thick skins like grapefruit, avocado, and bananas.

The Environmental Working Group (EWG) ranks popular food items every year based on the amount of pesticide residues that were discovered on them. The "Dirty Dozen," a list of the 12 fruits that should only be bought organically, is something they publish. They also produce the "Clean 15," which are secure and are available at standard retailers. To view their most recent lists and choose where to focus your organic food budget, go to www.ewg.org.

Using less pesticides Choose fruits and vegetables, especially those that are less susceptible to pests, so that they can survive with fewer pesticides. The vegetables in this category are onions, broccoli, cabbage, and asparagus.

Animal Products Usage Laws restrict the use of antibiotics, extra hormones, and human growth hormones in organic meat and dairy products. It is advisable to get in touch with the relevant authorities to find out whether the business or market you are buying from is truly organic. Reports on dairy and eggs are published by the Cornucopia Institute on its website (www.cornucopia.org). Another place the EWG suggests people turn to for organic dairy, meat, and other products is the Organic Valley Family of Farms, a collection of more than 1,300 certified organic farms spread over thirty states.

Have you heard of it?

When choosing organic food, health always comes first. According to a Nielsen Company study, 49% of respondents said they buy organic products because they think it is better for the environment, while 76% of customers worldwide stated they do so because they think it is healthier.

Extra Points

Do you currently buy organic products? Here are some suggestions to help you do that: Produce markets: You may help local farms by buying their products at farmers' markets and cooperatives in your area.

CSAs: The best organic food is produced by local, in-season farming. Taking part in a Community Supported Agriculture (CSA) program is a great way to get year-round access to seasonal, in-season food from neighbouring farms. CSAs provide "shares" to the public in order to supply seasonal food directly to the customer. Shares typically consist of vegetables but may also contain meat and poultry. Members receive weekly produce boxes as part of their contribution. Visit www.localharvest.org to locate a CSA in your area.

The phrase "Homegrown" If you own a home with a huge yard, start producing your own fruit and keeping a few chickens for fresh eggs. This will let you control the process of growing your own food. Learn the right methods for raising and feeding hens, and be sure to use non-pesticide methods to manage pests, weeds, and other issues.

Eat Less Dairy

Ice cream is necessary on a hot summer day.Cheese in your omelette; milk in your cereal. Dairy has probably been a staple in your diet if you're fortunate enough to not be lactose intolerant. And for good reason—it is rich in calcium and protein. Unfortunately, whole dairy products contain a lot of saturated fat. Too much whole dairy may be harmful since saturated fat is a lipid that should be avoided, as we learned in Week 11—Read the Box.

The good news is that you don't have to completely give up dairy in order to change to a healthier diet. You may easily cut six grams of saturated fat and more than fifty calories from each glass of milk by switching from full to low-fat milk. You could cut eight grams of saturated fat and sixty calories per cup by switching to nonfat or skim milk. Making just one small adjustment could result in weight loss of five to six pounds within a year if you typically drink a glass of milk every day.

More good news: all dairy products, including yoghurt, cheese, and even ice cream, can be altered with this straightforward alteration. Making the switch might be incredibly beneficial for your body if you often drink dairy. Switch to fat-free or low-fat (1%) dairy instead of whole-fat dairy.

What Can You Do If You Have a Lactose Intolerance?

You may be lactose intolerant if consuming dairy products causes you to experience cramps, gas, nausea, or diarrhoea. Lack of the digestive enzyme lactase, which is necessary to break down lactose, may make it difficult for you to digest lactose, a natural sugar found in milk. If you are lactose intolerant, you might still be able to eat dairy products.

Beginning with milk and milk products with less lactose, there are several products available for people who are lactose intolerant. Nearly 70% of lactose-intolerant patients report less digestive issues after having dairy with a meal, according to Dr. Michael Martini of the University of Minnesota

Department of Food Science and Nutrition. This is due to the male's role in enhancing digestion by lowering lactose absorption into the intestines. The degree of lactose intolerance varies among individuals. Lactose intolerance that is extreme is a rare condition.

Due to their low lactose content, most people with lactose intolerance can consume fermented foods like cottage cheese, yoghurt, aged or hard cheeses, as well as other animal milks such as goat milk and sheep milk, without experiencing any problems. The ability of intestinal bacteria to adapt, as discovered by additional study, enables lactose-intolerant people to tolerate up to eight ounces of milk each day.

Other Calcium Sources

Since dairy is one of the best sources of calcium, a vitamin crucial for bone health, it is acknowledged as being a necessary component of a balanced diet. The FDA recommends that consumers consume 1000 mg of calcium per day, which is found in one serving of skim milk at 30% of that amount. The following foods are excellent sources of calcium in addition to dairy, which is one of the best sources:

1. 3 ounces of canned, bone-in sardines contain 325 mg.
2. After being boiled and drained, one cup of collard greens has 266 mg.
3. 1 cup of cooked and drained spinach has 245 mg.
4. 3 ounces of pink salmon in a can with juice and bone contain 181 mg.
5. 12 cups of cooked and drained soybeans provide 120 mg.
6. 197 mg are present in 1 cup of cooked and drained turnip greens.
7. Nutritiondata.com is the source

An approach to success

Many consumers complain that low-fat dairy tastes watery or avoid it because they are worried about the flavour. Like most things, it all boils down to your habits. If you currently consume whole-fat dairy products, you can use these straightforward methods to acclimate your palate to low-fat or even nonfat dairy:

What about milk? You could wish to switch to the level of milk with the least amount of fat today, depending on the type of milk you frequently consume. If you typically drink whole milk, for example, start the week with 2% milk. Alternately, if you now consume 2% milk, switch to 1% milk. Your taste buds won't be alarmed by this alteration because it is so mild. Change to the next decreased fat level after two or three days. The milk you should be drinking should have no more than 1% fat.

Yoghourt: Numerous well-known brands of yoghurt are already nonfat or low fat. If you've been eating full-fat yoghurts, switch to low-fat yoghurts. Try Greek yoghurt if you prefer your yoghurt to have a richer, creamier flavour. Even when it is plain, Greek yoghurt is creamier and richer than regular yoghurt. Because it has more protein and less sugar than regular yoghurt, it also provides better nutrition ounce for ounce. Try plain unflavored yoghurt and add your own fresh fruit for a much healthier alternative if you usually consume yoghurt that has been sweetened or has fruit on the bottom.

Cheese: Low-fat types are recommended because fat-free cheese typically has an unpleasant, rubbery flavour. Fat-free feta cheese, which typically has a pleasant texture and tastes great in omelettes and salads, is the lone exception to this rule. Part-skim mozzarella, reduced-fat cheddar (shredded or standard), and reduced-fat Swiss cheese are a few delectable low-fat cheeses.

If you consume ice cream frequently, think about switching to low-fat frozen yoghourt. If eating ice cream is a special delight for you, by all means, reward yourself.

Coffee: Switch to whole milk if you want to add cream or half-and-half to your milk. Reduce the amount to 2% once you're used to drinking full milk in your coffee. Work your way down to 1% milk eventually.

Have you heard of it?

It is estimated that between 30 and 50 million Americans have a lactose intolerance. In contrast to the 60%–80% Ashkenazi Jews, 50%–80% Hispanic Americans, 95% of Asians, and 100% of Native Americans, just 2% of people with northern European heritage are lactose intolerant. However, this figure varies significantly by race. However, inter-racial unions are reducing these figures.

Extra Points

Already regularly consume low-fat dairy products? Consider switching to nonfat dairy and skim milk to up the ante.

Make Healthful And Encouraging Ties With People

Relationships that are solid and encouraging are crucial for our mental health and wellbeing. According to studies, those who maintain positive relationships are happier and less stressed than those who do not. Healthy relationships actually have a bigger impact on our health than things like food, exercise, stress, smoking, drugs, or even genetics. A study in the American Journal of Epidemiology found that people with strong social and community links had a two to three times lower risk of dying young than people with weaker ties.

The Preventive Medicine Research Institute's founder Dean Ornish, M.D., and the author of Love and Survival: The Scientific Basis for the Healing Power of Intimacy argue that when we feel alone and isolated, we are more inclined to make bad decisions for our health. They also hinder our ability to completely enjoy life's positive aspects. However, love, intimacy, connection, and community are restorative and can improve our happiness, sense of purpose in life, and overall health.

Have you heard of it?

Living a solitary and isolated life, regardless of activity, raises the risk of disease and early mortality from any cause by at least 200–500%. Create strong, empowering connections and keep as far away from damaging ones as you can.

An approach to success

Each link is valuable or at least has the potential to be valuable. With everyone, including friends, family, and even coworkers, you can develop a true bond. You can actively encourage the development of the traits that will improve your relationships' closeness, communication, and general well-being.

Quality Assurance Making useful connections pays off when you are aware of the traits you value in a partner and, subsequently, the relationship. List the characteristics that help you feel supported, loved, and respected. Then make a list of the characteristics that make you feel the exact opposite. While aggressively seeking out and forming connections with those who exhibit the former, minimise your contact with those who exhibit the latter. Even while you can't entirely cut them out of your life, you should make an effort to minimise your encounters with people who aren't encouraging, who make fun of you, or who don't share your values.

Offer and Acknowledge: Building strong connections requires participation from all parties. It is equally crucial for you to actively participate in building and maintaining connections as it is for your friend or loved one. If not, the connection is imbalanced, which will inevitably lead to dissatisfaction and disdain. It shouldn't always be a one-way street, even though there will undoubtedly be moments when one person depends on the other more than the other and vice versa. Allow your family and friends to support you as well. Don't just stand by them.

Likewise with others Any relationship with the intention of being supportive needs to be founded on mutual respect, trust, and honesty. If you want the other person to trust you, you must be trustworthy in return. It's also crucial to be sincere while letting others be who they are. Finally, remember that showing kindness and respect to others may aid in earning their esteem. Respect for one another is essential, even if we periodically disagree with our friends or family members.

Practise Good Habits: Relationships change throughout time, and maintaining a healthy one requires effort. To believe that you'll never experience challenging times or circumstances with the people you care about is naive. The most crucial factor is how you respond to certain circumstances. Consider putting some of the following actions into practice to establish and sustain successful relationships:

Healthy Communication: You should speak out politely and openly when you're unhappy in a relationship. Avoid negative attitudes or behaviours that could lead to resentment or harm, such as the silent treatment or carrying grudges.

Engage in active listening to demonstrate a sincere interest in what others are saying. Each partner must feel valued and free to speak openly and honestly about significant issues for a relationship to be healthy. Take the time to truly comprehend one another. So that you might more fully share one another's lives, actively assist one another in conquering difficult situations and conditions.

You need to be able to forgive since no one is perfect, not even you. They will eventually let you, your loved ones, and friends down. You must return the kindness in kind, just as you would want people to overlook your flaws if they were theirs.

Dependability: While it's true that occasionally unforeseen circumstances prevent us from fulfilling our duties, disappointing people frequently demonstrates that we don't value them or their requirements enough to be trustworthy. In addition to looking for allies who will, you should maintain your word and your commitments.

No-security bonds There is nothing more annoying than a person in your life who only shows up when they need something or are asking a favour, and then disappears once those requirements are addressed. Instead of just hanging out with people because they can help you, try to discover friends who you actually enjoy being around. Find friends who appreciate you and your friendship without being rude when they do so without offering anything in return.

Extra Points

Already skilled at building trusting relationships in your personal life? If you engage with harmful or risky connections, it will advance. Limiting your contact with toxic people is advised because of their potentially harmful effects on our health. If you can't break off your connections with someone altogether, try to lessen their bad influence. Here are a few advices:

Do the toxicity maths. Negativity and harmful relationships frequently coexist. Someone is toxic if they make you feel horrible about who you are, what you do, or who you are as a person. Poisonous traits can be displayed by people who are clever, narcissistic, critical, envious, disrespectful, or dishonest. In an effort to bolster their own egos, people with toxic personalities regularly do harm to others.

Try to make things right. Try to discuss your issues with the toxic individual if you value them. Share your concern for them, your relationship with them, and your awareness of their shortcomings. Declare that you wish to look for ways to make your connection stronger. You might be able to save the relationship if they are open to it. It could be time to move on if they are not.

Define Your Boundaries Clearly. Unfortunately, poisonous connections may arise with anyone, whether they are close family members, colleagues, or lifelong friends, making it challenging to entirely get rid of them. Limit your interaction with them at these times and set clear boundaries. Tell them that even though you care about and love them, you don't want to be around negativity if they cross your boundaries or do something inappropriate. Tell them you can't be around them if they can't be positive or respectful.

Bring in people who are hopeful. Have you ever had a friend who gave you energy, made you feel special, or gave you more self-confidence? You are better off because of people like this. There will be less room for negative people in your life if you surround yourself with more inspiring, upbeat people. If you keep up your positive connections, the detrimental impacts of toxic relationships will be less noticeable.

Get Rid Of The Portion Distortion

Many of us have a tendency to underestimate how much food we actually eat while overestimating suitable portion sizes. It shouldn't come as a surprise given that portion sizes have increased steadily over the previous 20 years to the point where we've entered a period of "portion distortion." Restaurants and fast-food companies deliver obscene portions in an effort to provide the client with "super" value. Businesses have enormous packaging for their goods at the grocery store, and even at home, we've managed to gradually increase the size of our crockery. It is horrible that our propensity to think and consume tremendous amounts is reflected in our waistlines. All this expansion has obviously had an effect on our waistlines.

Knowing how much to consume is a key ability that is necessary for weight loss and maintenance. Additionally, when we eat in moderation, we are able to eat until we are full without going overboard to the point that we will feel bad later. Learn the appropriate portion proportions for the meals you consume, and practice portion management on a regular basis.

Have you heard of it?

According to a study, Americans typically underestimate their daily caloric intake by up to 25%.

An approach to success

You must learn two things in order to estimate the proper meal portion sizes: Both the quantity of a typical food that comprises a portion size and the way that portion size is visually depicted must be understood.

The listings that follow show pictures of everyday items that illustrate the serving sizes and portion sizes for several food categories. There are an endless amount of processed or packaged foods, thus with a few exceptions, the majority of the items listed are whole foods. Given that emphasising whole foods is frequently recommended over emphasising processed meals, doing so also looks more appropriate.

Have you heard of it?

Plates had an average diameter of 10" in the 1980s. The typical plate size today is 12". According to Dr. Wansink of Cornell University, people tend to over serve themselves when given a larger plate. However, eating from the smaller plate can lead to consuming 22 percent fewer calories. A normal adult could lose 14 pounds over the course of a year by switching to a smaller plate size if a regular supper on a 12" plate includes 600 calories.

Purchase measuring spoons and cups if you don't already have them. You might even want to think about utilising a nutrition scale to weigh different foods. In order to have a good understanding of average portion sizes and what they consist of, measure your food consumption this week and compare it to the visual signals. So that people may easily access some kitchen essentials, display them. You might want to bring a few of them with you when you go out to eat. Without measuring cups, spoons, or any other tools, you will ultimately feel at ease calculating portion sizes and be able to do it anywhere.

An eating area

When we eat out, it could be particularly difficult to consume moderate amounts of food. Consider ordering two appetisers rather than an entrée to put the servings in perspective. You might decide to divide the entrée and the appetiser while dining with friends. When ordering an entrée for yourself, decide how much of it is a portion size, and then put the extra food in the refrigerator. You have two options: request a doggy bag or give the food to someone else. Dessert is generally shared as well.

Build up

Although the idea of strength training might bring up pictures of huge, monstrous men, it is a practice that may be advantageous for all of us. The improvement and maintenance of muscle tone are two of the most obvious advantages of strength training. Lean body mass increases and body fat decreases when muscle mass does as well. Additionally, we can increase our metabolism by up to 15%, which will enhance the efficiency with which our bodies burn calories.

Maintaining a healthy weight and a trim figure depends on this. The advantages go well beyond just seeming advantageous. Once we reach puberty, we start losing 1% of our bone and muscle mass per year. If the lost muscle mass is not replenished, it will unavoidably convert to fat. The loss of bone and muscle, on the other hand, can be slowed down, stopped, and in many cases, reversed through strength training.

This protects against degenerative conditions like osteoporosis and arthritis. Ligaments, joints, and tendons all function better after strength training. Flexibility, balance, and coordination are enhanced; as a result, there is a potential 40% reduction in the risk of injury and falling. According to study, strength training increases levels of good cholesterol, glucose tolerance, and insulin sensitivity while enhancing heart health and lowering blood pressure. Strength training releases endorphins similar to cardiovascular exercise that boost mood and have antidepressant effects, enhancing the quality of sleep and general wellbeing. Strengthen your body for 20 to 30 minutes every other or third day of the week.

An approach to success

Before beginning a strength-training program, consult your doctor as you would with any exercise program. So that you may correctly incorporate activities into your program, discuss with her any ailments or vulnerable regions. To master the correct form and technique for strength training, which are crucial for avoiding injuries or torn muscles, if you are new to it, you may wish to work with a personal trainer for a few sessions. They'll inspire you as you work out in addition to educating you about the different activities you might partake in.

A certified personal trainer will also make sure to create a training plan that is effective, safe, and appropriate for your needs. Look for programs at gyms that include weight or resistance training, such as Body Pump or Body Sculpting, if you cannot afford or do not wish to employ a personal trainer. These can be excellent starting points for fundamental strength training and ought to be sufficiently difficult, especially for beginners.

Strength-training Techniques

There are several ways to exercise your muscles. Make sure to select a form or forms that you are confident you will continue to like. Enrol in a class if you prefer to take classes versus working out on your own. Start with some books or weight training DVDs if you're a private person who loves to work out alone. Keep the following more popular varieties in mind when choosing the strength exercise you are most interested in:

Workout Lifting Weight training is a method for building muscles that involves lifting weights over their whole range of motion, either using weight machines or free weights (such as dumbbells or barbells). one of the easiest forms to pick up and implement into a training program.

Interval/Circuit Training: This type of exercise combines strength training with aerobic and endurance training to maximise the benefits of both types of training. Strength and aerobic exercises should be done together to increase training efficiency and increase muscle endurance.

Exercises involving weights. Instead of using any equipment, your body serves as the weight and resistance in this kind of strength training. You can work out every muscle in your body with this method. Push-ups, pull-ups, belly crunches, and leg squats are examples of common workouts. This kind of strength training also includes a variety of Pilates and yoga modifications.

Exercise for Strength: By employing resistance bands, weights, or devices (like those found on Pilates equipment) to push, pull, stretch, or bend against resistance while in the water, you can build muscle. The easiest and least expensive kind is without a doubt resistance bands, which are thin tubes that provide resistance when stretched. Normally, you can find them online and at any store that sells sporting items.

Isometric exercises involve holding weights or providing resistance while being still in one posture for an extended length of time. When utilised to focus and strengthen muscles at a certain joint angle, this format performs well.

Exercises that involve high-intensity motions like bounding, jumping, and hopping are known as plyometrics. Plyometrics is a very efficient form of strength training since it aims to stimulate more motor units than usual. Since it improves speed, strength, and explosive power, the majority of sprinters, jumpers, and throwers incorporate it regularly into their training programs.

A Strength Training Program's Foundation

When beginning a new workout regimen, practice caution. Exercise tiredness or, worse, damage might arise from overextending yourself too quickly. To become acquainted with the exercises and routines, start with lighter weights or less resistance at first. Use larger weights as your comfort and confidence grow. Whatever strength training method you use, the majority of exercises include the following:

Preparing and calming down Any exercise session needs to begin with a warm-up and end with a cool-down. Your body needs to warm up before exercise and cool down afterward for your heart rate to return to normal. Static stretches for the muscles you intend to work out after five to ten minutes of reasonably strong cardio exercise, such as walking. Before continuing with more static stretching, perform at least three minutes of low-intensity aerobic exercise after cooling down. (For a list of stretches, see Week 10—Take Time to Stretch.)

Instances and Sets: Every exercise in strength-training programs, especially those that involve weight lifting and resistance training, often follows a set/repetition format. A set is a collection of repetitions, whereas a repeat, such as a bicep curl, is one complete motion of an exercise. Eight to fifteen repetitions can make up a set, and many regimens may include two to three sets of each exercise.

For muscle growth, eight to ten repetitions are typically ideal, while twelve to fifteen repetitions are excellent for toning. However, start out easy by performing one set with 12 to 15 repetitions. According to a study, performing a single exercise twelve to fifteen times with the recommended weight is equally as effective as doing it three times.

Adding to or removing from: It's important to use the right weight or resistance when doing resistance or weight training. Choose a weight that will make you feel exhausted after twelve to fifteen repetitions in order to determine the appropriate amount to employ. Every set you perform ought to contain a challenging last repeat. Increase the weight or resistance after you can complete fifteen repetitions of an exercise without difficulty.

As many repetitions as you can till your last one is quite challenging when utilising your own body weight. Acute pain shouldn't happen, even though some degree of muscular soreness after exercise is normal. Stop the action if you experience any pain while performing it. Additionally, you may have overdone it if you experience joint swelling or intense muscular soreness after working out.

The advantages of sleeping: As vital as working your muscles is resting them. Strength training makes your muscles get stronger because they are ripped during exercises and then repaired during downtime. They continue to break themselves apart and rebuild, which makes them stronger. It's crucial to give your muscles enough rest so that they have time to recover. It is recommended to give a muscle forty-eight hours of rest before working it again.

You may choose to work out your full body two to three times per week, preferably on Mondays, Wednesdays, and Fridays, to give your muscles the rest they require. Another option is to alternate between different muscle groups when strength training each day. On Mondays, you may work on your back and chest while working on your arms, legs, and other body parts on Tuesdays and Wednesdays, respectively. In either case, make sure to give each muscle group the recommended forty-eight hours of rest.

Observing Outcomes You might be curious about how quickly you might experience benefits if you're new to strength training. You may see increases in your strength and endurance as well as greater muscle definition in as little as a few weeks if you stick to the recommended two to three strength training sessions per week, lasting twenty to thirty minutes each. You will, however, receive out of it what you put into it, just like you would with anything else.

Milton Keynes UK
Ingram Content Group UK Ltd.
UKHW020630021023
429777UK00015B/799